Bounce Back Better

10 (+1) KEY STEPS FOR BUILDING RESILIENCE

· ·

CARON ASGARALI

BALBOA.
PRESS

A DIVISION OF HAY HOUSE

Scripture taken from the King James Version of the Bible.

Balboa Press books may be ordered through booksellers or by contacting:

Balboa Press
A Division of Hay House
1663 Liberty Drive
Bloomington, IN 47403
www.balboapress.com
1 (877) 407-4847

Print information available on the last page.

ISBN: 978-1-5043-6856-8 (sc)
ISBN: 978-1-5043-6857-5 (e)

Balboa Press rev. date: 11/18/2016

CONTENTS

The Conceptual Framework

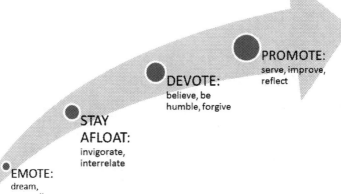

PROMOTE:
serve, improve,
reflect

DEVOTE:
believe, be
humble, forgive

STAY
AFLOAT:
invigorate,
interrelate

EMOTE:
dream,
mourn, live
momently

FOREWORD

Raymond S. Hackett

T HE 1970S, THE 1990s, and even now, 2016 have unleashed a wave of economic, political, and social change in Trinidad and Tobago. As a result citizens – young and old – have developed a craving for sudden and unlimited wealth. Indeed, people no longer seem to want to be followers. Everybody now wants to be a leader, earning great incomes. Along with this new aspiration, has come the demand for certification – the gateway to high-income jobs.

Against the background of the wave of social change and attitudes, identified above, Caron Asgarali has given us a participant observation account of the consequences of wanton crime. Not only did she simply give an account of her misfortune, she also provided advice with respect to how others, who may be unfortunate as she to experience a similar fate, can respond to the trauma of medical and social recovery. Indeed, she even has gone beyond this. Her book advises on a number of social imperatives – how to develop the necessary discipline for coping with overwhelming misfortune; how to manage a scientific approach to eating for good health; how to build character and integrity; and how to identify with God or the Supreme Force of the universe.

I have known our author for at least ten years. She at one time was my reticent but diligent and brilliant postgraduate diploma student who, when she spoke or shared an opinion, was always informative and to the point. Never, during my interaction with her in class, did I imagine that our paths would cross again after graduation. However, for reasons beyond my comprehension, Caron Asgarali, some years after graduating from my postgraduate programme in educational administration, approached me to assist her to write a book on clinical supervision of teachers. She completed the book effortlessly and subsequently invited me to work with her to conduct clinical supervision workshops in schools. Unfortunately, I was unable to assist her with these workshops.

The point I wish to make with the preceding paragraph, Dear Reader, is to have you understand the dimension of Caron Asgarali's philosophy and personality. Without doubt, she had developed an approach to life which is immersed in educating people and adding value to their lives. She started with her book on clinical supervision to help teachers enhance their levels of professionalism. After her misfortune, although caught up in the trauma of recovery, she decided to share her experience of life with others in a second book. Now she has gone even further to serve in her third book as a messenger for recovery from misfortune and tragedy, a motivational speaker, a nutritionist, a dietician, an amateur psychologist, a modern day philosopher, and in so many more roles you will discover for yourself.

As an educator for the past five decades and three years, I cannot honestly admit that I have read a book more comprehensive than and relevant to the times as Bounce Back Better 10 (+ 1) Key Steps for Building Resilience. Inspired by the message and advice which characterise this book, I look forward to an outcome which will cause the general public, magistrates, judges, lawyers, members of the Lower House and the Senate of our Parliament, policemen, doctors, nurses, social workers, probation officers, teachers, particularly secondary school students above Forms One and Two, guidance officers, clinical psychologists, and last but not least advocates of Restorative Justice to read this third book which Caron Asgarali has written. Without doubt, it is prescribed reading for all.

Too many of us live in Trinidad and Tobago, the region, and indeed the world, unable to empathize with victims of crime and individuals who have fallen victim to abuse and hard times. Caron Asgarali's book, I have absolutely no doubt, will help you, Esteemed Reader to develop a rational perspective on and an understanding of what people, traumatized by criminal and social circumstances, experience. If you yourself have been a victim, be assured that this book will help you to bounce back better on to the road of recovery.

Raymond S. Hackett

Educator and Educational Consultant

PREFACE

I N THIS LIFE we are constantly bombarded by the "successes" of others. Great fanfare is the order of the day when an athlete wins a gold medal or when a favoured sports team emerges victorious. Remember the celebrations when President Obama first won the Presidency? What about all the hype surrounding such award shows as the Oscars or the Emmy awards? ... And this is all good. It has its place and purpose. But we must be cognizant of the scope of success.

Each of us experiences success in different ways, sometimes every day. Sometimes it may seem as though defeat has locked us in its dentate grip. That is the time when we must allow our internal light to begin to shine. The overcoming of life's difficulties or misfortunes is not a task for the faint-hearted. No, it is a feat which requires the courage of a matador, the discipline of a soldier and the strength of a lion, underscored by the patience of Job. The ability to face our internal battles head on with the conviction that we will not get lost in the deluge of despondency is equivalent to, if not greater than, any tangible reward.

There is no obstacle to success for anyone, as long as there is commitment, passion and constant motion. According to Newton's Law of inertia, there is a tendency for objects to remain in their current state. It requires some external force to cause a change in that state, whether it is a state of motion or a state of rest. How does this relate to success and tragedy? Well, if we regard our misfortunes as obstacles, then we can sit back and refuse to move. If, however, we embrace them for what they are – external forces meant to change the direction of our lives – then we can use unfortunate circumstances to propel us along a path of forward motion in a positive direction.

I have so many times referred to the incident which changed the course of my life – the incident which resulted in my possession of a "bionic" jaw and a new look. I refer to it once more. I could have wallowed in self-pity or drowned myself in a sea of desolation or become immersed in a state of ennui. Through the grace of God, the flexibility of resilience and neuroscience, not one of those scenarios has happened. When I was shot at close range by a cold blooded hoodlum, it brought my life to a complete stop... before I began once again to march, this time slowly but steadily, to the rhythm of life.

Given an assortment of trials – a disfigured face, bouts of depression, several surgical procedures, being on extended leave without pay, depleted savings, no car, retirement on medical grounds, outstanding mortgage payments... I reacted in a way that was considered uncharacteristic for me by my relatives. I was able to adopt a positive outlook as a result of acceptance of and adaptation to my circumstance. I was able to draw on a strength which everyone else seemed to think I had innately, but which actually was a consequence of surrender to God's will. The external force of that incident brought changes in the direction of my life.

I have since found a new passion. Actually it was a hidden passion, recently discovered. I love to write and so I have spent many hours putting pen to paper as the old saying goes. My inspiration for writing is divine. My purpose is God's purpose. This book was written out of a compulsion to share the knowledge and skills associated with resilience that I have developed or learnt out of that unfortunate incident.

The introduction outlines the difficulties encountered out of that defining moment; it traces the ways in which I was able to renew vigour for life and provides the framework for a system to develop the resilience needed to overcome any type of challenge anyone of us may face. Each chapter is one step in the system that worked for me in being able to bounce back better, even as I am still a work in progress. The chapters end with practical applications and key learning points for each step. Within the book I have incorporated references to scientific literature related to some of the steps. Initially, I had included only ten steps. The eleventh step came during the editing period. It was a practice that had become so ingrained in my approach to life that I almost overlooked it.

The greatest benefit from using this book will be gleaned by following the steps as outlined. As you read a chapter, it is best to carry out any associated exercises in tandem so as to begin creating new neural pathways. Using the book in this way will encourage and accelerate the process of reprogramming your brain for forward motion. However, as I may have alluded to, several times in the book, self-awareness should also be your guide. You alone know your strengths and weaknesses. You will know what aspects of your journey, through the dales of life, need prioritizing in order to begin the trek to life's peaks.

If you are currently in the midst of a difficult time or have been through a trial, I congratulate you for having survived to this point. By taking the time to read this book you are already displaying at least one sign of resilience: you are looking to supplement your toolkit of resilience practices.

A major breakthrough in bouncing back better is recognizing that external assistance may be necessary sometimes. Asking for help is not a sign of weakness. On the contrary, it is a sign of great courage and wisdom. I have immersed myself in much reading. I have asked for help from family and friends, as well as from professionals, but in the end the responsibility for my upward or downward swing remained solely in my hands. This book, therefore, is testament that no trial is too great to overcome.

As you read this book if you wish to share your burden or joy at overcoming or just want to reach out, I would consider it an honour and a blessing to hear from you. My contact information is at the back of the book. You will also find the title and details for my other book and the title for the upcoming one.

All the best as you climb onto your personalised trampoline to begin bouncing back better.

Caron R. Asgarali

INTRODUCTION

"Acknowledge and accept what was;
be at peace with what is and;
move forward into a brighter tomorrow."

THOSE WHO KNOW me or who have read my first book, From Lion to Lamb A Spiritual Journey, would know that in January 2013 I was seriously wounded by bandits in an attempted robbery. I was left depleted physically, emotionally and financially. Thankfully my mental capacity was not diminished and my spiritual journey was catalyzed by that "defining moment" to quote Mr. Philip G. Rochford who wrote the foreword of that first book.

It was a traumatic time; a time fraught with fear of what the future would hold. There were so many uncertainties, so many surgeries to undergo and so many changes and challenges. How could I move on? Where could I start? Could I begin to save my life again, physically, psychologically and financially?

Writing my last book and getting this one published are testament that I could and I did! It was not easy but I did it. Do I take credit for having done it all on my own? Never! There was no way I could have done it alone. The question then is this: how does one move on from such a dramatic setback?

Before I share how I was able to bounce back successfully from this disadvantageous position, permit me to divulge the depths to which this incident had brought me. This may provide a better perspective for those who may not have read the first book. It may do so also for those who did read it but may not have grasped or considered the full effect of that episode on my life.

The Physical Setbacks

For those who knew me and had heard of the shooting, the physical damage could only be imagined. Many persons had only read or heard about the incident. Few persons had been allowed in the Intensive Care Unit at the San Fernando General Hospital where I had spent the first three days after the incident. After being transferred to Ward 8 (the Ear, Nose and Throat ward), my brothers screened well-wishers, allowing only those they considered closest to me to visit.

Seeing me today, one can only express superficial sympathies for what had happened. After healing, plastic surgery and then more healing, the wound and subsequent scar belie the extent of the injury. This makes it quite easy for the unsuspecting to believe that it was not as bad as was reported.

Even when I first wrote about it, I do not think I conveyed the true extent of the damage. My chin was completely blown away! There was a gaping hole at the front of my face and what was left was fractured from ear to ear. Embedded within the lower portion of my face, downwards from the eyes, was shrapnel from the exploding bullet and the broken car window. There were also bone and teeth fragments from my chin and jaws, scattered like sprinkles on an iced cake.

The resulting appearance is best understood if I share this little story with you, a story that the persons involved possibly would not even remember.

One morning at the hospital, after I had been transferred from the ICU to Ward 8, I awoke to the sound of shuffling feet and papers. I opened my eyes to find myself surrounded by a group of doctors. Now, you have to remember at that time, I was still under the influence of strong painkillers; I still had not seen myself and; I could not speak. There were tubes inserted almost everywhere and large bandages covered my face. I imagined myself looking like some alien from a Hollywood movie.

The pupils of my eyes drifted from left to right, as I counted about six doctors around the bed. I soon found out that they were plastic surgeons. It was a mixed group of male and female doctors who, to my damaged self with a nightmarish image of my face, all seemed to be the most gorgeous persons I had ever seen. There was a pregnant silence which was abruptly broken by the words, "What do they want us to do? There is nothing we can do for this one." That sight of those fresh, clean faces, along with the devastating blow of their words, intensely magnified the dismay I had been feeling.

God alone knows how I did not give up at this point. I remember telling my friends and family afterward that, for some reason people seemed to believe, since I could not speak, I could not hear. Remarks and comments were sometimes made that led me to this conclusion. Surely the doctors did not make such a statement, deliberately, for me to hear!

Despite these sentiments expressed by the good doctors at that time, they later agreed that it would be possible for reconstructive, plastic and cosmetic surgery. (On a side note, I promised my friends to get a movie star makeover but it was not meant to be.) The reconstructive and plastic surgeries would take place later in the year, after having my jaw re-broken, wired, unwired, re-broken and re-wired. The breaking each subsequent time after the actual injury was done because the jaw was collapsing inwardly as it healed, distorting the shape of the mouth and interfering with the alignment of the upper and lower jaws.

In the approximately seven months before reconstructive surgery, my diet was limited to liquids only. That was surprisingly not too difficult except for the times when everyone else was feasting on some of my favourite foods as I passively sat and watched. I remember when my nephews spent the entire afternoon with me as we prepared Buffalo wings with seasoned wedges. We followed a recipe and added our own "Trini" style seasonings. The result, I heard, was fantastic. Wings were being tasted before we were finished cooking all of them. Of course, I could not sample any.

The only foods I enjoyed blended were callaloo (which is blended anyway) and lentils. For those who may not know, callaloo is a local Sunday lunch staple. You may read more about it on my blog at https://educater.wordpress.com/2015/11/22/building-blocks/. One day shortly after being discharged from the hospital for the first time, we held a thanksgiving service at home. The menu was curried chicken, dhal, pumpkin, mango amchar (a spicy hot dish of cooked mango slices), curried channa and aloo (as we refer to chickpea or garbanzo beans and Irish potato) and paratha ("buss up shot" or roti). The aroma of that spicy meal was so tempting that I decided I was going to eat. I blended all the curries and dhal and drank it like a soup. It did taste delicious but there was no way I was going to have my regular meals blended.

Blending tended to change the taste I was accustomed to, the taste I expected and the mouth feel. It also ruined my appetite. The nutritional drink, Ensure, became a staple for me as did ice cream. I could have as much ice cream as I wanted then without gaining weight! Even with ice cream as a main course, I was soon so thin that my pants were doubling up on me. My weight dropped to eighty eight pounds. I was only aware of how small I had gotten because of the way my clothes fitted. I could not see the way it made me look because I could only bear to look at my eyes when I looked at myself in the mirror.

After reconstruction, I lost a little more weight but soon I began to eat soft foods and then gradually by December 2013 I was eating almost everything once again and, of course, my nemesis, those protruding pounds, began to accumulate. However, it would be just over two years after the incident, sometime in 2015, before I would start looking and feeling healthier.

Reconstructive surgery left me with scars on my left shoulder, hip and thigh. The details of surgery may be found in my first book. My mouth was closed in by approximately thirty percent. This left me with an overbite which reveals, what I consider to be, a startling, scary smile. In spite of the variety of changes I had to undergo physically as a result of a criminal act, I am thankful for having made it through that difficult time. However while the physical setbacks were immediate and obvious, the emotional storm was yet to come.

The Emotional Setbacks

Through the grace of God who designed the human body to withstand forces greater than we can ever imagine, my mind dealt with the injury in phases. I was able to undergo rapid physical healing partly because my mind directed all its energies into that aspect of recovery. I will talk more about the rapid healing in the chapter on training. However, soon after the bulk of the physical procedures were over, my mind shifted focus. The emotions began to get out of control.

I remember clearly the day I went to the National Insurance Board (NIB) office in San Fernando, South Trinidad. That morning, a friend had accompanied me to meet someone who may have been able to give me some information regarding collecting NIS payments. Owing to what I consider some serious slip ups on the part of the Ministry of Education, I was in a somewhat sticky situation. My salary payments had been stopped in August 2013. I had been unaware of that until October 2013, although I had called to enquire about my status in September. At that time, I was reassured that, payments were still being made and that they would call me as soon as any changes were instituted.

This meant I needed now to put things in place so that some financial remuneration would be obtained. The lady to whom I was sent was pleasant and sympathetic. I was referred to her by one of my brother's friend. All she asked was, "How are you feeling? Tell me what the problem is." As I started to answer her, a tidal wave of emotion swept over me and I felt the tears bursting forth from the reservoir where they had been corralled for the past nine months.

In the middle of the busy NIS office, surrounded by the lady and my friend as well as many other clients, I could no longer keep the flood gates closed. My entire body wept. I struggled with every fibre of my body to control the flow of tears but to no avail. I left the building still in tears. I cried even as we walked to the nearby car.

For what was I crying? Everything and nothing is the best answer I can give. There was no one thing that caused it. It seemed that having completed the physical healing, the emotional healing was just beginning. That was amazing to me because I thought I had emerged unscathed. I had been handling the situation magnificently...or so I thought.

That event had happened on a Friday morning. The following Monday morning, I had to pay my usual visit to the doctor on the ward at the hospital to obtain a signed and stamped sick leave. Driving to the hospital with my mother that morning took all the control I could summon. I felt like screaming out aloud. I felt like letting out all the hurt and pain I was feeling from some obscure, unknown place deep inside of me.

Instead I sat in silence, as rigid as a rock, gripping onto the car seat with all my might, as if holding on to something physical was restraining my inner demons. Thankfully, we soon arrived at the hospital. I left the car with a curt thank you to my mother and a reminder that I would call her when I was through. I hurried to meet my doctor knowing that I would need to have professional help, given all the other symptoms I had been experiencing.

There had been many restless nights. So many times I had been overcome with emotion, on the verge of tears but I had never actually cried, except for one time when I was still at the hospital. That time my father's sister, Susan, had come to visit. She was so overwrought at the sight of my condition that both she and I began to cry. I cried because of the pain I thought she was feeling because of me. The next major crying would have been that day at the NIS office. But although crying had been scarce, there were other indicators that emotional coping was not as good as I had thought.

I had been experiencing episodes of wanting to scream and shout just as I had felt in the car with my mother. I had flashbacks of the scene, the pouring blood and even the scent of the blood. There were nightmares from which I awoke bathed in perspiration and struggling to breathe. When I did fall asleep, I did not want to get up on mornings. I did not want to leave the comfort and security of my bed and blanket. I did not want to see anyone or talk to anyone. Then there were those ever threatening cold tentacles of fear surrounding me whenever I was stuck in traffic or when I heard fireworks.

That Monday morning, as my doctor casually enquired about my welfare, he unwittingly released the catch valve on the gates which secured my emotions. Everything came out. With trembling voice and blurry eyes, I confided some of what I had been going through. He referred me immediately to the hospital's psychiatric clinic.

By the following week, I was at the psychiatric clinic. I met with the doctor in charge and spent about an hour with her and a young doctor. The younger one had been present on the night I was admitted after being shot. I tried to get some more information about my condition that night but was unsuccessful. At the end of the session, I was diagnosed with Post Traumatic Stress Disorder, given a prescription for anti-depressants and referred for counselling by a social worker.

I gladly took the drug. The thought of breaking down in front of strangers was not a comforting one and the intensity of the desire to shout and scream was too much for me to hold back on my own for much longer. So I went on drugs, prescribed drugs! While the drug may have done its job, in my humble estimation, the counselling was invaluable.

The social worker to whom I had been assigned turned out to be a past student of a school at which I had taught before this incident. As I began to speak with her, I started to cry uncontrollably again. I could not understand this crying thing. I was always a strong person. Tears would come but not for me. I cried for persons who were disabled or disadvantaged, I cried for animals or babies and anyone or anything that was in pain. I sometimes cried in anger. But I did not cry for me. What was happening?

To this day I am so grateful for that social worker. She handed me some tissue and in a very soft, sweet voice reassured me that it was okay to cry. But, more importantly, she reminded me that she was a past student of the school at which I had been teaching for the last seventeen years of my teaching career. We had spoken on several occasions, although I had never taught her.

Graciously, she complimented me on a range of perceived strengths and gradually got me to calm down. At that point, she volunteered to hand my file over to another social worker. She offered to do so in case I felt uncomfortable confiding in someone whom I knew. I declined the offer because she had already made me feel a lot better and had instilled in me a sense of confidence in her.

The combination of medicinal and psychological therapy, coupled with exercise, worked for me. Within a relatively short time I was on the road to emotional recovery, and soon after, I would write and publish my first book. Psychological trauma is inextricably linked to any sort of crime or violence perpetrated against someone. It is not always immediately evident but it is definitely anticipated. However some of the insidious effects of criminal activity extend beyond physical and emotional setbacks

The Financial Setbacks

Not only had I been physically damaged by bullets but my car had sustained quite a blow too. The entire left side of the car received bullet holes; one was very close to the gas tank! The front left window was completely shattered. There was blood confined to the front left side where I was seated that fateful night.

My first business upon getting out of the hospital was to have the car removed from the premises of my ex-husband. He had been kind enough to keep it there until he felt I was capable of having it relocated. The car had to be sent for a body job. That was my first major bill after the incident.

The next step was to arrange to sell the car. My younger brother handled that for me and executed it perfectly. So my first financial loss was my car. The money from the sale of the car was put into the bank for use in paying the bill for reconstructive surgery. All other savings, salary and incoming money went to that fund for surgery. My friends, as I already related in my first book, From Lion to Lamb, held fundraisers and many well-wishers gave generously.

After the surgery my resources were limited. I no longer had a monthly income, although I was still employed by the Ministry of Education. By the following year, in March, I was called in before the Medical Board and retirement on medical grounds was recommended. I agreed to accept it. By September 2014, I was surreptitiously told, by someone seeking my interest that a permanent replacement had been sent in my position. This occurred even though I had not been informed officially that my retirement was accepted. In fact, I was not officially told of my retirement until late December 2014 and I only signed a letter of agreement sometime in January 2015. The outcome is that I was now unemployed with no income since August 2013.

Now, please permit me to divulge some of the not so obvious financial effects of this crime, to which I had alluded in the previous section. A lot of money was spent by the State for:

- treatment upon arrival in the emergency room
- emergency surgery and all its accoutrements
- my stay in ICU and all relevant personnel, medicines and supplies
- treatment and care on Ward 8
- psychological treatment and counselling.

Granted that the actual time of my stay was significantly less than what was first suggested, the cost would have still been significant.

Below I have listed some of the resources utilized as a result of that single criminal act committed against me. These would have further added to the burden of the State and an already overcrowded, under-stocked hospital and overworked staff. Here is a partial list of resources needed to look after this one patient:

- doctors, nurses, nursing assistants, cleaners and maintenance workers
- nutritionist, specialized feed formulation and regular blood tests to monitor my nutritional needs
- a physiotherapist
- X-ray personnel, the photographic films and the mobile equipment brought to me when I could not go to the X-ray department
- dental scans that had to be outsourced to private dental clinics
- an ambulance and driver as well as an accompanying nurse to take me for the scans
- the almost endless list of supplies including painkillers, antibiotics, gauze, bandages, tubing for the tracheostomy, syringes, antidepressants, anaesthetics, clean linen…
- psychiatrists and social workers

It must be highlighted that the list is not exhaustive. It does not include the cost and resources used at the private hospital. Can you begin to imagine the enormity of the bill for just one patient? Thankfully, I did not have to dip into my savings for treatment at the public facilities. Not so luckily, at the private hospital, I did have to deal with the financial strain of a hefty bill and a salary reduction, then a salary elimination and eventual retirement.

With savings depleted, having been used for reconstructive surgery, with no source of income, and retirement still unofficial, the full extent of the incident is now becoming a little clearer. Now, I had to deal with the depth of emotion that accompanies sudden and unexpected loss of assets and the accompanying loss of concept of self that is intrinsically linked with an injury to the face and the loss of a job, particularly when tenure at the job was in excess of twenty years. The daily challenges, the nightmares, the flashbacks, the financial constraints and the social stigma, real or imagined are outlined but the reality was so much sharper and detailed. Again the question arises, how ***does*** one overcome in the face of such adversity and begin to bounce back better?

Moving Past Setbacks

The great thing about this life is that obstacles are just as intimately a part of it as are the good times. Each time we encounter an obstacle and overcome it, we emerge stronger, better and more capable of dealing with the next one. The challenging part of such encounters is in knowing where to start and how to get to the next level.

The analogy of computer games is appropriate here. I have not really played a game for a long time but I do know that games are designed with various levels of achievement. To move from one level to the next, one has to combat or defeat an obstacle and emerge a winner at the lower level, acquiring a certain amount of points or lives or skill to move to the next level. So too in life we move through levels acquiring strength, courage, resilience, skill and experience to the very end before moving to the highest level.

Just as we defeat enemies or obstacles along the game in a systematic manner, so too we move along life's journey by systematically rebounding after each setback. The keyword here is **systematically**. In casting a backward glance, I have recognized that I did have a system. My system worked for me in managing the pain and trauma of a major setback and has continued working for minor challenges along the way.

But let me not get ahead of myself. Let me show you the ways in which I have bounced back better from what was a devastating blow.

Bouncing Back Better

Two months after I began going for counselling and medical therapy, I mustered the strength, through divine inspiration, to write my first book.

Mr. Philip G. Rochford graciously agreed to do the foreword. In July 2014 the book had gone through the stages of editing, typesetting and formatting, proof-reading and publishing. Between July and September 2014, working with a self-developed marketing plan (amateurish by any standard), I was able to get the word of my book out and create a bit of a buzz. I began with television interviews by the major local stations. This was followed by newspaper articles. The actual book launch took place in September 2014.

Following closely on the heels of the television interviews I got my first speaking engagement. It was a disaster! I was invited by a local insurance company to be the feature speaker at their Christmas Breakfast Morning. I thought that speaking would have been easy for me since I had taught for so many years. I was nervous in spite of those years of experience. I had a speech planned and was intent on speaking from the heart. I was overcome with nervousness and I read the speech instead of talking to my audience. Needless to say I did not capture the crowd. I did not connect with my audience.

I persisted with the speaking and did not turn down any invitations. One significant engagement was an interview at the Canterbury Retreat and Convention Centre at Oveido, Florida. The event was hosted by their Christian Chamber of Commerce. The experience was fulfilling and successful. I sold books and made contacts as a result of that session. The most recent speaking engagement, at the time of writing this book, was one that I had solicited through one of the Rotary Clubs in San Fernando, Trinidad. The event was the commemoration of their 111th Anniversary and their World Peace and Understanding celebrations.

Some of the speaking was paid and some was not. I accepted any offer to speak as long as I was free at the time. The idea was to gain more practice so as to keep refining and improving my delivery. Although the income from speaking was minimal, it helped because, as I have already noted, I no longer had a steady job. My great concern at this time was to ensure that I had sufficient funds at the end of each month to meet my mortgage commitments.

To compensate for the loss of income, I accepted any part-time work for which my physical presence was minimal. I worked with CXC (the Caribbean Examination Council) as a moderator for the School Based Assessments in Chemistry. I worked inputting data at one company then I started working with an IT (Information Technology) company. The second job allowed me the flexibility I needed: I could work from home, having to make personal appearances at scheduled times only.

Before beginning the second job, I started giving Chemistry lessons after school hours and on Saturdays. The times were good for me because talking for long periods was still uncomfortable. It also worked because my speech, although good most of the time, became a bit garbled when I got tired.

So, income was being generated through physical and online book sales, the odd speaking job, the part-time IT job and the lessons. The ball was once again going upwards! Still very small incomes but, as I always say, I was never one with extravagant needs.

At a personal level, I trained for and completed my first ever half marathon in August 2015!

The System

So how did I move from being physically, emotionally and financially depleted to competing in a grueling race, telling my story on a national and international level and becoming relatively successful with managing my financial situation after a severe, unanticipated loss?

Upon careful examination of the last three years a trend of behaviours has emerged. This trend I have observed not just in moving past that critical situation but also in being able to overcome minor challenges along the way.

As I have already mentioned it is a systematic method, initially subconsciously applied but, soon enough, one which has deliberately become an integral part of recovery from a variety of degrees of challenges.

There are ten essential steps. These steps are all important; no step has more value than another; they work synergistically with each other. The steps I have listed are based on the premise that healthy bodies are required to develop healthy minds which in turn give us ultimate control over our lives.

Though the system has at its core ten steps, there is one other step that plays a pivotal role in the establishment of all the other steps. It brings to mind that contemplative figure, sitting with his chin upon his fist ensuring that his life is worth living. The daily practice of casting a backward glance upon the day just ended, throws an illuminating glow of understanding on actions taken or not taken both by self and by others. Thus although the system is listed as having ten steps it would be incomplete, perhaps even ineffective, without incorporating the elements of examination and analysis. So, having reflected, I am compelled to include this additional step.

The Ten Steps of the System (and the bonus step): The Game Shifter!

1. Be Goal Oriented. — **G**oal setting
2. Feel, Grieve and Accept. — **A**cceptance through grieving
3. In Crisis, Live in the Moment. — **M**oment by moment
4. Develop Physical Stamina. — **E**xercise and things physical
5. Seek Support. — **S**eek Support
6. Function in Faith. — **H**onour God
7. Be Humble. — **I** after you
8. Be Forgiving — **F**orgive
9. Continuously strive to improve. — **T**rain the brain
10. Practice philanthropy. — **E**mbrace giving
11. Be reflective — **R**eflect

The source from which energy dissipates in water is found at the center of a series of concentric circles. Your faith, whatever you determine your faith to be, should likewise be placed at the center of your philosophy and your existence. In this way, the energy of resilience will be generated from a central focus within your psyche and emanate equally throughout your being to aid in holistic restoration. Based on this premise, I have included honouring God or having faith as the sixth step of the system, with five steps before it and five after. The steps before are not meant to diminish the importance of faith but rather to re-enforce the centrality of faith to physical and psychological healing.

The human capacity for pain and discomfort is tremendous. We are capable of withstanding great pressures even more than our physical bodies appear to be able to withstand. One writer compares our potential for dealing with pain to that of a bamboo bending in strong winds but almost always springing back, resisting the force of breaking.

You have that capacity too! You can be flexible, not yielding to turbulences pulling and tugging in all directions, with great force. You can move past each new obstacle because you have the determination, courage and faith to take control of your life and bounce back better. Adopting a systematic approach, gradually picking up the pieces left after a crisis situation, may assist in helping you to overcome major or minor challenges along your life's journey.

This system, the Game Shifter, contains simple steps that we all use at one time or the other. The power of the system lies in being able to bring all the parts together, concentrating their effectiveness. Some may wonder why not use the more common term, Game Changer. Perhaps it may sound more potent or more popular. However, an important point to note is that making incremental changes, particularly during times of trauma or crisis, may be easier to achieve than radical changes. Additionally, a shift in behaviour could translate into significant emotional and intellectual alterations.

Consider the Leaning Tower of Pisa. The Tower now leans at an angle that has been adjusted over the years since its construction. The top of the Tower is about 4.5 metres displaced from the vertical. This means there is a slight displacement at the base of the Tower that manifests into an amazing tourist attraction at the top and a phenomenon of physics. Regardless of the reasons behind the leaning of the Tower, the result is undisputable. A slight shift is sufficient to create a wonder!

The name, Game Shifter, was adopted based on that line of thought. Gradual, manageable shifts in attitude, approach and behaviour may help smooth the path through adverstiy and make bouncing back better possible. It does not deny the benefits of radical changes in less adverse circumstances. It simply stands on its own merit of being the system that worked for me as I wandered through unknown paths before being able to adapt, adjust and advance forward.

The chapters that follow will examine each step of the Game Shifter in more depth, providing relevant experiences to illustrate its benefits.

Step 1

BE GOAL ORIENTED

"Create purpose. Set long term goals."

IN AUGUST 2015, I completed my first 13.1 mile race, my first half marathon. People who do not run always make the same joke about running half a marathon: "Did you get tired and could not run the whole marathon?" Having been a runner for many years, I was always curious to know if I could run 26.2 miles. The longest distance I had ever run in a race was 5kilometers. I may have run longer in training but in challenging myself, I never ran more than a 5K.

When I heard about the half marathon organized by a local insurance company in my country, I was immediately drawn to it. It would be the stepping stone to doing a marathon. If I could complete 13.1 miles then surely I could push myself to complete 26.2. I had just about two months to prepare for the half marathon. I had been running regularly before that and would run for about an hour on evenings.

To be able to compete in the half marathon I would have to be able to stay on my feet for at least three hours. I had to have a precise schedule to ensure that I could complete the race. My time was limited. My body was just getting back some strength and my stamina was now being re-established. I had my challenges but I was determined to enter that race!

My **goal** was set: completing a half marathon on the 31st August, 2015 starting at 5:30 am from the roadway in front Atlantic Plaza in Couva, Central Trinidad.

It was now clear **what I wanted to do, the day** I would be completing it, **the time** it would start and **where** it would begin: all the elements needed to set a goal.

Having made that decision and set that goal, I now had to come up with a training schedule to execute it. The training would have to be tailored to get me moving, walking or running, for three consecutive hours. At this point I was concerned with finishing, not with finishing in a certain time but in finishing the race, period. I would not spend much time on speed training but would focus on endurance training.

With the invaluable assistance of a good friend, who is knowledgeable in training techniques, I was able to work out a step by step plan based on the number of weeks before the race. I had to include sufficient rest days because it was not going to be easy to train towards a three hour goal, especially at my "tender" age.

As the race day approached my training sessions tapered. On the day of the race, I felt prepared. I was a bit fearful that I may not have been able to go the full distance. However once the race began that fear dissipated. The fear was replaced by the glory of the morning, the exuberance and energy of the other runners and the endorphins being produced that caused me to feel ecstatic.

Completing that half marathon was a great accomplishment for me. First, I proved to myself that I have what it takes to run 13.1 miles: discipline, endurance and perseverance. Second, it meant that I would be able to complete a marathon, 26.2 miles, as long as it was something I really wanted to do. Completing it was a test of my mettle, it was not a race against anyone else; I simply had to compete against me, my will power. It taught me a lot about the sacrifices necessary to achieve: the waking up at 2:30 or 3:00 am to ensure I ate and digested before going on a long morning run; foregoing get-togethers so as to get in afternoon training sessions and; making more healthy food choices.

As I mentioned, there were times when my training had to be done in the morning and at times it was done in the evening. This became necessary although I had planned the schedule for evening runs. When unexpected, unavoidable events arose, I had to be flexible in my training times to make sure that I got in all the training I needed each week.

There were people who felt that they needed to give me advice on how I ought to train, what times I should do it, why I should not over-train and so many other hodge-podge of ideas. I would smile politely and take note of what was offered. However, ultimately I was the only one who could know the capability of my body and what was best for me in the long run. After ruminating on the various bits of advice, I would adjust my routines if I deemed it necessary or discard the idea if I did not consider it beneficial.

This undertaking revealed some steps that I had already adopted in other areas of my life. A pattern had begun to emerge and I was able to capture that pattern to share with anyone who wants to achieve a goal or stick to a plan.

It is important as you set out in life, seeking to be successful in your endeavours, however you may measure success, that you develop a general life plan. This life plan is what most of us refer to as our dreams. We must have dreams, big or small. What may be big for you may be small for someone else. The idea is that having a dream or a plan for where you want your life to go, means that you can focus your energies into making that dream come true.

The overarching dream in your life, where you ultimately want to end up, directs the decisions you make in life concerning education, your job, your spouse, your home… every aspect of your life is covered by the big dream in your life. The canopy of a tree has a definite shape when observed from afar. That shape on closer examination is a result of many limbs and branches spread out in different directions. Your overall dream is similarly shaped by many smaller dreams which come together to give definition to your base desire.

To get on the path to achieving your dream requires that you put those smaller dreams into place so as to create the matrix which could support your life dream. A matrix by definition is the starting point for something else. Everything has a starting point. Success for each of us is the achievement of our great life plan. The starting point for success then is the achievement of each of the smaller dreams.

WHAT DOES IT MEAN TO BE GOAL ORIENTED?

Being goal oriented can be outlined as follows.

Have a general dream or life plan. Visualise this dream. See yourself as having already accomplished this dream. After carefully determining the steps you need to take in order to accomplish your major life goals, then you may support that goal by breaking it down into a series of finely tuned specific goals.

There are many good books and short courses designed to teach how to set goals. That is not the objective here. Here I just want you to be aware that you ought not to drift through life only waiting for the right wind to blow to steer you in whatever direction it may be heading. Instead you need to take control of the reins of your life, have your main goal as your focal point and set about taking small steps leading in the direction of your dream.

Setting goals for supplementary projects for your main goal is important; how you set these goals is vital. The SMART method is used in goal setting; your goals need to be:

Specific; Measurable; Attainable; Realistic; and Timely!

The beauty in having a plan is that you are always moving forward to your final destination, as long as you take those baby steps. Some may argue that it precludes spontaneity. I humbly submit my disagreement with that view. Instead having these smaller plans leading toward the ultimate goal, caters for spontaneity. You would have a degree of flexibility which would still allow you to work steadfastly toward your goal. You will easily recognize when a particular action is not working in your favour. You would be able to change the plan according to your circumstances at any time, should any obstacle arise and still be on course for the larger picture.

More than that, setting goals puts you in charge of your own destiny. It gives you the control to accept or discard the ideas that other persons may put forward to you. What you want for your life and the actions you are taking to achieve this may be at odds with what others perceive to be the best thing for you. Be kind and gentle; listen to alternate points of view then use wisdom, passion and purpose to guide your choices. After all, it is your journey, is it not?

Before we leave this step in the system, let me share with you one final story which so beautifully illustrates the principles in this step.

When I had submitted my first manuscript for publishing, I started reading more avidly about the next steps that I needed to take as an independent author. I realized that I had started to write without having a clear pathway for the ultimate distribution of the book. Recognising that, I began to read even more about what needed to be done. I needed to have a marketing plan in place so that when the book was finally published people would know about it and buy the book. If people did not buy it, then my message would not get out and I may have well not written the book.

I researched on marketing plans until I found a template that was fairly simple to follow, easy to execute and with which my style of work was compatible. I spent the time that was recommended, detailing what I had to do, whom I needed to contact, when I needed to do it, how I was going to do it and any other relevant information. Soon enough I had a plan that included beginning to spread the word to family members and friends, contacting bookstores, television stations and newspapers.

That plan was a great blessing without which I may not have had the kind of visibility I had prior to the official launch of the book. The book may not have been a best seller (yet) but it gained a lot of exposure for me and for sales. By the time I was ready to launch, I was meeting people in the grocery, at the market and in other stores who recognized me from the interviews either on television or the newspaper. One person even contacted me to speak with her group out of those promotions.

The point is that I had a vision or goal. I designed a plan of action to achieve that goal, detailing what had to be done as well as establishing timelines and deadlines. Then I executed the plan which resulted in the successful achievement of that goal.

Similarly, you too can develop a dream. First you articulate that dream, then you break it down into medium and short term goals. Finally you establish a series of action steps that will help accomplish those goals and ultimately your big dream. Dreams may be constantly improved or upgraded by the opening of greater possibilities as smaller goals are completed or adjusted to be in alignment with your purpose.

Goal Setting Exercise

1. Spend some time contemplating, and then write down your big dreams or long-term goals.
2. Break down each major goal into a series of smaller steps that are necessary to achieve that goal.
3. What are your strengths: skills, traits or knowledge that you already have to help you achieve that goal?
4. What are your weaknesses: skills, traits or knowledge that you need to acquire to better position yourself to achieve your goals?
5. What factors may prevent you from achieving your goals? Are you afraid? Are you financially challenged? Are you constrained by relationship expectations?
6. What possibilities may arise to catalyze your process of achieving your goal? Did someone offer you a part-time job? Is there a sudden need for your particular skill?

Key Learning Points

1. Have a dream (long term goals).
2. Break the dream down into a series of smaller goals.
3. Establish timelines and deadlines for each small goal.
4. Be flexible with smaller goals without losing focus on the main goal.

Step 2

FEEL, GRIEVE, ACCEPT

"The canvas of your life is splattered with pain and hurt.
Feel, grieve and accept your challenges to initiate a new perspective."

WE ARE CONSTANTLY faced with situations that take us out of our comfort zones or catapult us into despair. It may be attending a function alone, not knowing anyone else there… or being an introvert. Or it may be losing a job or the prospect of losing a job. Perhaps you are awaiting the results of a medical examination. As a result, you play a variety of scenarios in your mind: "Maybe I have cancer…or diabetes… or high blood pressure…or a heart condition"… and the list goes on. It could be the devastating news of the death of a loved one. Divorce may be on the horizon. Maybe you left home blissfully unaware of dramatic circumstances that would soon unfold: a robbery or an accident involving serious personal injury.

Such negative news can be received personally; alternatively it can be relayed by different types of messages (written, text) or by a telephone call. It can be obtained through a newspaper article or a television programme or even via the Internet. Whatever the situation is, it can take you out of that sphere of life with which you are most familiar and which you are most capable of handling.

If you are a fan of athletics you may be aware that when winning times for certain events such as the sprints, hurdles and long jump, are announced, mention is made of wind reading. There are two categories of wind reading: a positive reading resulting from a "tailwind" or a negative reading resulting from a "headwind". A "tailwind" is one which assists the athlete. It exerts a push from behind the athlete and enhances his performance. Up to a given maximum, a "tailwind" is legally accepted; beyond that maximum value, the result is illegal and does not count for record purposes. A "headwind" creates resistance for the athlete. The athlete moves in one direction while the wind blows in the opposite direction. All headwinds are considered legal.

One day as I was running I was reminded of these two terms: "tailwind" and "headwind". That day I ran along a different route, not my usual run. As I ran around a roughly rectangular field I realized that running in one direction around the field, I faced a mild tailwind. Running in the opposite direction left me feeling as though I was in a hurricane zone: the headwind was tremendous. I was being pushed backward almost literally (perhaps not eating properly at that time could have been a contributing factor).

What was I to do? I could have stopped running. However, that would have upset my running goal for the week. I could have tried to push harder to keep moving at the same pace. This would have left me depleted and unable to complete my daily running goal. I could have adjusted, and did adjust, my stride so that I was able to move more slowly along that portion of the field with the headwind. In this way, I was able to accomplish my goal and save some energy by adapting to the conditions along the different areas of the track.

When we are dealt circumstances that upset our equilibrium in life, what do we do? Do we stop doing all that we set out to do? Do we pretend that we are superhuman and fight and struggle unsuccessfully against these upsets? Or do we adjust our internal meters, reset our goals and circumnavigate the obstacle? To be able to stand tall, with your character strengthened and your dignity maintained, I suggest that it is best to select the last option.

Initially, you may have to stop doing some activities which become beyond your new capacity. You may need time to come to terms with the situation. The time needed for grief and eventual acceptance of the setback is unique for each individual. This is an essential step before anyone can overcome any type of challenge. Some persons need very little time; others need days, weeks, months or years. It does not make you inferior to someone else if you need more time than they appear to need.

Instead, as was illustrated in the fairy tale, Cinderella, no one else can fit exactly into your shoes. Your inherent traits such as your personality, your experiences, your beliefs, your values and faith, your position in life and your resilience are some of the factors which determine the size and shape of your proverbial shoe. Science is now finding evidence for a secondary, chemical-based system that works along with the main central nervous system for relaying messages throughout the body. This secondary system uses large molecules to translate emotional experiences into physical symptoms or signals. This means that emotions are not experienced only in the brain but they may also trigger biochemical reactions in almost every system in the body. It supports the mind-body connection; what affects the mind does seem to affect the body.

Thus there is evidence that we should not allow anyone to minimize our grief or the time we need to heal after a traumatic experience. We have to be prepared for such challenges and go through a process of grieving, customized for our unique situations. There is one catch though; while grieving is important, if it becomes an obstacle to healing, then professional help will become imperative.

However, once you are past the grief stage of a trying experience then acceptance of your current situation will step in and you will be ready to take responsibility for reassessing and resetting your goals. The real challenge is not in avoiding the hurdles of life but in being able to recognize them for what they are: catalysts of change. It is being able to embrace obstacles that stand in the way that you selected for yourself and using them to propel you onto another path. Great insight is gained when the curved ball thrown at you is used to your advantage. The greatest gain comes when you are able to discern that the ball was curved to divert you in a different direction, deliberately.

A curved ball sends you on a spontaneous journey; a journey that is unplanned and unknown. Such a journey could be postponed if you live in denial of the circumstances created by your trouble or trial; postponed but not cancelled. Rest assured that no matter when you do decide to embrace the challenges of life, you will once again resume the journey for which you are called. I see it as a cycle: we face challenges which help us to mature spiritually, emotionally, mentally and physically; this maturity then helps us to cope with further challenges. The cycle is repeated until the final destination of our life's journey appears on the horizon.

It has been said to me that people must not accept what has happened to them. The tone and manner in which it was said belittles acceptance. Acceptance is not an evil; in fact in times of pain and distress, acceptance is a critical factor for being able to move forward. Resilience requires acceptance. Resilient people come to terms with their situation, no matter how difficult it may be. They are able to use the pain as a catalyst for progressive movement.

Research has shown time and again that in psychological suffering, brought on by a wide range of factors, there is a higher level of functioning associated with those who are willing to feel their pain (Hayes & Smith, 2005). One way to consider this is to draw an analogy to swimming against a tide. In struggling against a current, energy is expended unwisely; the swimmer may end up depleted and eventually cave in to the force of the current. However, if the swimmer moves with the current, a place and time may come when he will be able to get around that current and move to safer ground.

I can convey only some depth of the trauma I experienced that fateful night I was shot. Societal ills have peaked to such an extent that people have now come to view a shooting as a routine part of criminal activity. However, the terror, the pain and suffering cannot, and ought not, be minimized. My life was being threatened; I faced and almost literally bit the bullet. A torrential downpour of warm blood was released as my face exploded when the bullet penetrated.

That was only part of the hurdle I would be facing. As I have said there was much more to it than that. There were the months of not being able to eat; the weeks of not being able to speak; the months for physical recuperation and; the reality of having lost my job, my savings and my car and the depression that constantly threatened to take control.

As I was transported to the hospital, I pondered on so many things: how would my son react to this news; how would my family feel; how would my once closest friend cope with the news; how was I going to overcome this hurdle; would I ever be able to look at myself again or be able to live with myself like this?

Through the grace of God I was able to shut those thoughts out of my mind. My entire being needed to focus on staying alive. Therefore, I could not dwell on negative thoughts. After the incident, while I was still at the hospital, I was able to think a lot about what had happened. I cried quietly. I imagined at times that it was all a dream. I did what I always did whenever I encountered difficulties in the past. I cocooned myself in a little world into which I did not allow anyone else and I hurt silently.

Whenever I carried out this practice of allowing myself to feel pain or anger or any hurt, I cringed inwardly. I isolated myself from others mentally. This I did by not letting them see the hurt I was experiencing, at least to the extent I was feeling it. At that time I could not let my mother, brothers and other supporters see how much I was hurting for they would not have been able to hold up and be able to help me. But inwardly I was feeling the extreme depths of despair.

This may sound as if I was doing myself an injustice. In truth, experiencing my suffering to the fullest was a form of therapy. This served to bring me to the point of being able to move toward healing. Not being able to accept negative occurrences in your life threatens to place you under bondage; a bondage created by a lack of forgiveness and holding on to the memory of what has passed. This may lead to thoughts of revenge against real or perceived hurts; it may even lead to the worst case scenario of suicide, a possible consequence of not being able to live with the pain of the past.

Consider, for example, the high unsolved murder rate in Trinidad and Tobago. Some cases were due to fits of rage and passion: a father kills a son; a jilted lover kills the focus of love. What causes such violent outbursts? There are many contributing factors working together to prompt these actions. One possibility is the reluctance to accept changes in circumstances - a love affair turns sour and the scorned one is unable to envision a life without his or her "reason for living" or relatives fighting over domestic matters which appear to be of greater importance than life itself. Those who lack the ability to accept the pain of adversity as a natural consequence in life seem to be unable to cope and bounce back from their loss.

On the other end of the spectrum, Trinidad and Tobago is blessed with strong persons who have faced and overcome extreme adversity. A well-known, somewhat controversial example is veterinarian Dr. Kryiann Singh. Dr. Singh was involved in a serious accident quite a few years ago. Badly damaged, he became wheel-chair bound.

No one would have held it against him if he had chosen to retreat from the profession and the inevitable public interactions. He could have allowed his situation to be the reason he did not do his job or take on certain jobs. Instead Dr. Singh turned that obstacle into a catapult and launched head on to establish his own veterinary practice, become a social activist and a senator. He was able to come to terms with what had happened, freeing himself of the shackles of the past. What a shining example of the power of acceptance in building resilience!

Among my personal encounters, I recall one of the most powerful illustrations of overcoming extreme adversity in a couple who lost their daughter through an automobile accident many years ago. I have always felt that there is no greater loss than the loss of an offspring. Really, how does one cope, far less move on after such an event? What I recalled, as a very young girl, was a couple who grieved. They grieved with class. We all knew they were hurting; their eyes bore an indescribable pain and emptiness. Yet, these parents were gracious enough to be polite and kind to everyone as far as was humanly possible.

They did not place a limit on the time they needed to grieve. It would be many years before the veil of pain was lifted ever so slightly from their demeanour. Their feelings of grief were manifested in their unique way. As a result, they were able to take the necessary steps to forge ahead for the sake of their remaining children. Yes! This couple exemplified resilience to me. They felt the intensity of their pain and used it to keep the momentum forward.

The ability to feel and the opportunity to do so are linked scientifically with healing and resilience. Those who experience emotion to its fullest are those who have the drive to push past suffering and hurt to emerge triumphantly through the fire of adversity. This pattern of behaviour has been displayed in cases of physical, psychological and financial setbacks. It is from this emotionally charged base that the passion for driving forward is born.

Conor Anthony McGregor is a mixed martial artist known for his fighting prowess, extravagant lifestyle and thrash talking. He gained international fame when he knocked out the then undefeated Ultimate Fighting Championship (UFC) featherweight champion, Jose Aldo in Las Vegas, Nevada, United States in December 2015. This defeat came about as he attempted to fight against Aldo who was much heavier than he was. His remarks afterward were that he had taken a risk, given it one hundred percent and lost but had no regrets.

His advice to his fans after this crushing defeat was brilliant and reflective of the mettle needed to have the resilience to come back stronger after a setback. He offered the profound advice that one must face challenges head on and never avoid challenges. He was onto something there. Facing defeat or difficulty, more so in an international arena, could destroy those who choose to allow it to have power over them. By holding your head up, accepting the fact that the carpet has indeed been pulled from under you and feeling the depth of the emotion of that loss, you position yourself on a figurative springboard for recovery and eventual success.

One of the problems with grief is that it is not always recognized. When it is, the grieving person may feel guilty about feeling so deeply. The thing is that grief is felt as a consequence of any loss, not only as a result of the loss of a loved one. It may be the loss of a job, the loss of savings, the loss of a house or car, the loss of a pet or the loss of anything for that matter. It is normal to feel when there is any type of loss.

The grieving process can be recognized by a combination of feelings which may include one or more of the following:

anger
guilt
self-condemnation
sadness
loneliness
confusion
an inability to think
sleeplessness or sleeping too much
avoidance of people, places or actions that you once enjoyed
crying
forgetfulness
an inability to believe that the loss really took place.

There may be other emotional manifestations of grief depending on the individual. These feelings must be channeled out of your being by allowing yourself to be immersed in them for some time, validating them, before throwing them off and getting ready to thrive once again.

In allowing yourself to feel it is also important to pay attention to when you begin to feel overwhelmed or when the weight of grief is becoming too burdensome. At such times it may be in your best interest to share your burden with someone else. It may be as simple as saying to a close friend or relative, "I just need someone to sit quietly with me." Alternatively you may turn to someone outside of your immediate support circle. You may feel a greater level of comfort disclosing more information to someone with whom you are less intimate. Perhaps professional help may even be considered and may be imperative.

Do not make the mistake of thinking about acceptance as giving up. Acceptance and giving up are on opposite spectrums of resilience. Acceptance means coming to terms with the loss you may have experienced. It implies acknowledging the extent of what has happened, neither do you enlarge its effect nor reduce the magnitude of how much it hurts. Instead you recognize it for what it is, you examine how deeply it hurts and why. In this way you will take away from the experience, the energy of emotion needed to propel you into a brighter future, knowing that there will be more obstacles but that if you can overcome this one then you are better equipped to combat any further hurdles in the event of life.

Along this journey of life, there will be good times and bad, happy times and sad and times of gain and times of loss. We have the option to allow the negatives of life to hold us back and keep us from enjoying future positives or we can learn to manage the pain of hurtful situations so that we can thrive forward. Harnessing the pain of difficulties entails taking the privilege of feeling intensely and grieving in a personal manner and time with the end result of acceptance to pave the way for growth.

Feel, Grieve and Accept Exercise

1. List situations that have brought you pain and hurt in the past.
2. Try to recall how you reacted to each situation.
3. Carefully detail any situation which may be currently causing you distress.
4. Write down how it makes you feel to think about this source of distress and pain.
5. As you allow yourself to feel hurt, pain and anger, do not allow those emotions to control you. Do not act in anger.

6. Redirect negative feelings by using your senses to feel positive: look at a sunrise or sunset; listen to music that you love or that relaxes you; infuse your surroundings with a calming aroma that appeals to you; eat your favourite food or dessert; stroke a pet cat or dog; feel a soft, warm blanket; or some alternative that soothes and refreshes you.

Key Learning Points:

1. Feel the intensity of your pain.
2. Grieve for your loss.
3. Use the force of your grief to push you to the point of acceptance.
4. Coming to acceptance paves the way to take another step.

Step 3

IN CRISIS, LIVE IN THE MOMENT

"Temporarily and deliberately adjust the lenses on your life,
adopting a slowed version of reality."

S ETTING LONG TERM goals is imperative. Having medium and
short term goals is essential to create the momentum for moving
toward those goals. In this way, small victories build confidence
and bring you one step closer along the journey to your ultimate goal.
However, in crisis times and in times of extreme adversity, the mission
to accomplish your goals becomes hazy. How do you focus on a goal of
jet setting around the world when you have just lost your job, a loved
one or when you find yourself on the receiving end of a disturbing
medical diagnosis?

When the burden of an affliction becomes so great that your future
grows indiscernible, then you have to take very small steps, carefully,
so as to be able to emerge polished by the sandpaper effect of that
difficulty. Such times require a buoyant approach in which tunnel
vision ought to come into play. In a dark tunnel you would hesitantly
but deliberately set out, step by step, gingerly feeling your way out. So
too crisis times are best dealt with by stepping out slowly, not able to
see too far ahead but step by step progressing from where you are to
where you want to be.

In my darkest times after the incident, looking too far ahead at my
projected life based on previously set goals became a deterrent to my
healing. How could I cruise into retirement, literally and figuratively,

when I had lost my job, my savings and my concept of self? Had I tried to recapture the goals I once had and used them as my beacon to a safe harbour, I would be still at sea. So, at hospital, my actions reflected my thoughts: gather my items to go to the shower before too many other patients went before me; have enough blank pages to write to my family and friends when they visited and; clean the tracheostomy with the use of the vacuum pump to prevent having to change the "trachie" tube.

Out of the hospital, the scope of my vision did not change immediately. I was still in a very trying situation. I was always focused on the next clinic visit. I had to clean the "trachie" every day, sometimes twice a day. I focused on drinking regularly; not just when I drank but what I drank. I tried to ensure my nutrition was not compromised as a result of not being able to eat solid foods. One of the most difficult matters was not being able to go back to school. I was torn between wanting to do better for my students and also not having the physical strength to last an entire day at school.

Many hours per day were spent in sleep. That sleep was an essential element in the physical healing process. Yet I chided myself for being lazy. Why did I not get up and do anything? I did not realize just how depleted I had become, and continued to be, as the healing took place and as I still could not eat solid foods. Each day became a challenge as I pondered what to "eat", when to sleep and what to do.

This changed when the date for reconstructive surgery was set. Now, I had a short term goal; from my perspective it was a massive step toward healing. Prior to reconstruction, I felt like a freak. Wherever I did go, I felt that everyone was staring at me. I sometimes saw people looking at me in, what I thought at best was pity and at worst was with disdain. It was difficult not to focus on what others thought when they saw me. I tried to be as inconspicuous as possible. I did not look directly at others and kept my head slanted downwards.

The anticipation of reconstruction provided a way to begin focusing once more on a short term plan and no longer on minute to minute details. I had to source funding. I had to get all supplies ready. I needed to obtain a walker for use after reconstructive surgery that included a hip graft. I needed to liaise with the insurance company to work out the details for payment to be made to the private hospital and to the doctors. There was a lot to keep my mind occupied and to distract me from diving too deeply inwardly.

Getting over the surgery was good for me in several ways. First it brought back a part of me that I had forgotten: the part that is headstrong, determined and willing to do what it takes to progress. It also improved the general shape of my jawline and made it possible to begin eating, albeit soft foods, once again. Overcoming the ravages of surgery paved the way for me to begin setting small, achievable goals on the road to healing.

The process of recovery was not smooth; neither was it direct or without pitfalls. Instead it was thwarted by the onset of Post-Traumatic Stress Disorder and many other twists along the way. Ultimately though, the general trend was positive movement in a forward direction. Each new obstacle in my progress brought me back to the point of living in the minute; struggling to survive moment by moment. The beauty in this is that consistently getting back in alignment with faith and a positive outlook each time I fell short, brought me ever closer to striving forward, closer to thriving.

Thus having been through my own trauma, I understand what is needed to be done in order to maintain sanity and to begin to cope with challenges in a meaningful way. To avoid being or becoming overwhelmed by stressors in your life; to be able to take the reins of your life into your hands after a testing period requires you to have a vision. You have to be able to see the larger picture, see your life five or ten years down the road; you must know where you want to head but … you have to be able to put it in perspective. Your big picture, your life goals have to be pushed into the recesses of your mind.

Now, this does not mean that you ignore your goals. No! You need to know where you are heading and what you want. You need to internalize your goals without having them looming directly and constantly in front of you as a reminder of what you have not yet done. They must be dangled from afar, enticing and alluring. In this way you will be able to break them down into action plans made up of many, smaller, less daunting, achievable tasks.

Take each day in stride and manage your time, emotions and stress level by focusing on daily tasks. Time constraints, heavy workloads and emotional burdens may seem to have put you in a quagmire. It does not have to be a dead end situation. You can turn things around.

When my life was taken out of my hands, in the face of what seemed impossible to defeat, I was able to gradually regain control. Step by step, I was able to rid myself of the suffocating stress of too much to handle, too little time to heal.

Focussing on Each Moment

As described above, I applied a very simple technique... I focused on each second; I lived minute by minute, hour by hour, day by day. I did not try to jump from being dependent on tubes, medications, doctors and nurses to being independent once again. In that way my mind was allowed to process only a quantum of information at any one time. The enormity of the situation and the urgency of time were not emphasized.

If you are feeling overwhelmed by time and burdens, I strongly recommend developing a routine. Human beings crave routine and habit. Routine is comforting and reassuring. You know what you have to do and without even thinking it gets done. Routine brings accomplishment. Each completed task speaks volumes about your ability to get things done, even under stress. Occasionally breaking a routine provides the thrill of adventure.

Until you have conquered your situation, having a routine is like having a safe harbour for a boat. There is security in being able to do daily tasks. It takes your mind off the negativity of the situation with which you are dealing. It gives you more time to analyze your situation and to bring back a sense of normalcy. It gives you back a level of control! For example, you could begin by starting each day at least fifteen minutes to half an hour earlier. Compel yourself to do this for three weeks, after which time it should become an ingrained part of your day. Use the time wisely: pray, meditate, exercise or do some work.

You may be thinking: it is easy to say this but how is it possible to do it when a crisis arises? How is it possible to avoid being engulfed by the burden of illness, injury or some other challenge? You may question: will I ever be able to complete a sufficient amount of small tasks to see the light of my greater vision? The resounding answer is that it can be done. I did it and so have many others. So, yes you can do it too. In fact, the relatively new field of neuroscience is finding more and more evidence that it can be done. Let me explain in simple terms.

Mindfulness

Imagine a large piece of land standing between where you are and where you need to be. You look for a path, but on finding none, you begin to walk through the untamed bush. As you make your way to the other side, you choose the path of seemingly least resistance. You wander from left to right, keep right, dodge a soft spot of mud, step over a large clump of growth, barely miss some garbage and soon enough you are on the other side.

Some days later you do the trek again, following closely the path you remembered taking. This happens several times over the next few months. Of course by this time, there is no need to try to remember where you passed because you have worn out a path that is now visible and easy to maneuver.

That is what happens in our brain. All thinking or cognitive processes, all emotional reactions, all behavioral responses and all physical functioning originate in the brain. The brain is a complex system containing many millions of neurons. Neurons are specialized cells designed to process and transmit messages via electrochemical responses. These tiny particles are linked together by synapses which allow the transmission of messages between neurons.

Groups of neurons form neural pathways or networks which are re-enforced each time we use that particular network. What this means is that the neurons change in response to a situation, creating a memory in the process. Each time we encounter that situation or something similar, the same network of neurons comes into play.

The more times we use a network, the more entrenched the network becomes. Ultimately the responses triggered by that particular situation, or one similar to it, becomes automatic. This means that unless the brain is deliberately re-programmed, you are going to be stuck in a loop of behaviors or reactions that have become learned. In other words, you use the beaten track of least resistance to move from point A to point B.

Thankfully, there is now growing scientific evidence to support a technique called mindfulness. Mindfulness was practiced by Buddhist monks and involves embracing the present, learning to observe yourself and your reactions in a detached way and as a result, adopting different responses to old situations. This is useful for dealing with habits which may be negative or of little value to us. It may help in better managing stress and trauma and all the accompanying physical symptoms. It could help develop concentration and focus and may be vital to being able to live moment by moment.

Mindfulness requires practice. It is not difficult to do but requires perseverance and discipline. It is so very easy to fall into autopilot reactions. Practicing mindfulness has helped me tremendously. Knowing that, scientifically, it has been proven to be sound, makes me more willing to stick with it. Having experienced positive results from indulging in mindful practice, I am now convinced of its worthiness.

Try this one technique today. If you get stressed out or frustrated or angry, focus on yourself. Feel the way your muscles tense, whether facial or neck or whatever muscle group is involved. Then gradually relax the particular muscle group. Feel the tension drain from your body and allow yourself to slip into gradual relaxation. Allow a smile to cross your face. Notice what you feel. If during this exercise external thoughts intrude, just acknowledge them before bringing yourself back to your relaxed position.

If you think about being angry or upset or any other negative emotion, remind yourself that it is just an emotion. It is not who you are; do not allow the emotion to control you. Instead you control it; it is just an emotion. Finally, remember to breathe and focus on your breath for at least one minute. Living in the moment and for the moment is a trait that resilient persons share. It is a useful tool for being able to move past difficulties.

We are all guilty of harbouring negative thoughts at times; some of us do it more than others. There are scientific links to negative thinking and physical and mental symptoms which demarcate ill health. Those who are constant worriers tend to build up the hormone cortisol in the body. Cortisol is commonly known as the stress hormone. Excess levels of cortisol and other stress hormones in the body are known to promote abdominal fat and weight gain, anxiety, depression, heart disease, sleep disorders and impaired cognitive functions.

On the flip side, there is another body of research on mindful awareness which has been linked to positive health effects which may include the following: physical effects such as lower blood pressure and improved immune functions; mental effects such as greater attention span, relief from anxiety and depression and improved brain functions; and emotional effects such as promoting well-being and addressing moodiness.

Mindful awareness involves being attentive to what is happening in the now around you; it requires an acceptance and openness to experience the present eagerly with the aim to acquire self-knowledge. The practice of mindful- awareness is at work during meditation, yoga, playing or listening to music, painting or other creative activity or simply spending time in the outdoors. These types of activities have been shown to help lower stress levels as we learn to direct our reactions to various stimuli differently from our norm in a more compassionate manner.

Positive Thinking

The unconscious mind is able to assimilate approximately 3 different ideas or concepts or observations every second or a total of about 60,000 in one day. Included in these thoughts is self-talk: the words we speak to ourselves during the day. These thoughts are not conscious but they are always present; they exert tremendous influence over our focus, actions, reactions and skills. Inherently each of us has a different capacity for the type of thoughts we process. Some people have a pre-disposition toward negative self-talk; some are inclined to more positive thoughts.

Prior to 1998 the field of positive thinking in psychology was considered to be frivolous; in 1998 an American psychologist, Martin Seligman assisted in providing scientific theory to substantiate this aspect of psychology.

Positive thinking has since been linked to many desirable health outcomes which include some of those listed below:

- More happy experiences which lead to lower stress levels
- Decrease in depression periods
- Better immune responses leading to less instances of the common cold for example
- Better management of cardiovascular disease
- General increase in life span
- Greater ability to deal with trials and challenges

Positive thinking was, and perhaps in some circles still is, scoffed at as a valid, scientific practice. Some schools of thought consider it similar to believing in fairies and unicorns. It is more constructively viewed as changing the manner in which you speak to yourself, to provide a backdrop of uplifting ways against which distressing matters or situations may be viewed.

It is generally accepted that a negative response to a challenging event or occurrence is cohesively bound to a lack of a panoramic view and focus of the said situation. When cornered in a seemingly hopeless situation, negative thinking results because the victim is rendered unable to discern a way out. Positive thinking does not mean that the hopelessness of a situation has to be ignored and that the victim must pretend that all is well. What it does mean is that a positive thinker will have a variety of responses for the same scenario; he or she will have a clearer grasp of the situation which allows for more logical thought to take place.

To incorporate positive thinking into our lifestyles, minute by minute, we need to pay attention to the words we speak to ourselves. Instead of focusing on minor issues we need to put on a different lens to see the bigger picture. Instead of only remembering the one mistake or misstep that was made for the day, we need to remind ourselves of the many successes we did have. Instead of thinking about the one extra piece of cake that you ate and how much weight you may gain, think about how lucky you were to be able to eat or that this now gives you even greater impetus to exercise. So you were moody today; no problem, you will have a chance to be kinder or more approachable tomorrow.

Positive affirmation is another good way to beat negative thinking. By telling yourself that you are a good artist, you direct your mind to acknowledge your ability and skill. By saying that the loss of your job now opens up the way for you to delve into entrepreneurship or network marketing or a new job, you do not minimize the loss. Instead you acknowledge the space created by the loss and direct your focus on filling that space. While positive thinking does not mean that you can think yourself into doing everything, it does ensure you are able to deal with a variety of issues using a repertoire of options rather than being self-limiting.

Negative thoughts act like a semipermeable membrane allowing only one type of physical response to a situation; usually this response develops levels of distress linked to states of ill health. Positive thinking is akin to a permeable membrane: many responses are allowed to combat the variety of problems life may present on a quotidian basis. It allows the body to cope with difficulties and recover quickly from setbacks, fertilizing well-being. Only you can make that decision to adopt the practice of positive thinking even in, or rather especially in, the midst of a crisis.

One final word on feeling, grieving and acceptance, depending on your particular situation, personality, emotional makeup, level of support and faith, you may not be able to cope with feeling and grieving on your own. I must stress the importance of seeking professional help at such times. Seeking help at your lowest times requires great strength. It is not a sign of weakness.

Live in the Moment Exercises

1. In times of crisis or adversity, slip into a slow version of reality; do only what is necessary in order to not feel overwhelmed: take medication, eat, seek counseling, exercise, rest.

2. Listen to others but do not immediately react or respond to their well-intentioned advice or suggestion.

3. Refrain from making hasty decisions. Defer major decisions to when you are more psychologically prepared or when the crisis period is over.

4. Make baby steps until in your estimation you are ready to leap into the new reality. Choose one chore that has to be done, that was not done the day before and do it.

5. As you gain momentum select one short or medium term goal and begin to work on it. List all the steps needed to achieve that goal and do them one at a time depending on your level of readiness and your external circumstances.

6. Establish a routine to develop security and reduce stress. Plan your days. Set a time to get up, at least fifteen minutes earlier than usual, preferably before anyone else is up. Use your time to pray, meditate, exercise or work.

7. Practice mindfulness. Begin simply. As you awake take the time to listen to the harmonious chirping of the birds as they welcome the new morning. Feel the cool morning breeze on your skin. Sit comfortably in a quiet place. Focus on your muscle groups, particularly those that feel tense. Gradually relax one of those muscle groups. Allow a smile to cross your face as you feel grateful for the morning. Acknowledge intruding thoughts but bring yourself back to your relaxed position. Breathe deeply, inhaling and exhaling slowly. Start doing this for at least one minute at a time until you can manage it for longer times.

8. Practice spiritual meditation. Pray according to your religion, focusing on scripture.

9. Play or listen to music.

10. Write down or say to yourself three things you did for the day that made you feel good about yourself.

11. Remind yourself of at least one thing that you are good at doing.

Key Learning Points

1. In crisis live by the minute.

2. Live in the moment until you are ready to take a small leap forward.

3. Sometimes it is possible to jump straight back into the routine of life. If this is possible then by all means do. If not, do not be hard on yourself; just keep trying, a little at a time until you are ready to do more.

4. Seek professional help when overwhelmed.

Step 4

DEVELOP PHYSICAL STAMINA

"Proper eating, drinking, fasting,
resting and exercise
provide the rejuvenation needed
to catapult beyond obstacles."

W E HAVE A spiritual, physical and social obligation to lead healthy lives. Our bodies are God's temples we are told; this underscores the importance of keeping our bodies clean and well-maintained from the inside out. We undergo the aging process naturally but we can take steps to reduce or slow down the physical processes which decrease our quality of life as our chronological age increases. Health challenges become a burden on finances, whether it is our own or that of our family members or governmental and employment agencies.

The new millennium has brought with it increasingly alarming figures of a variety of medical problems. These include but are not restricted to obesity, diabetes, coronary heart disease, high blood pressure and cancer. Psychological and emotional problems are also more evident because of being under constant stress and an increasing inability to cope with stress. The success of economies over the years means that there are many nations of wealth, with populations able to eat as much of whatever they wish to eat. Lifestyles have become more and more sedentary with the associated decrease in physical activity. Perhaps there is a lack of knowledge of health related matters or a lack of conviction or discipline or perhaps people just do not care about their health as they should.

The reason or reasons for not being more committed to a healthy lifestyle is or are important. However, regardless of the why, it is time now to take stock: age or gender is irrelevant; now is the time to start a health awareness programme or; now is the time to renew your commitment to be conscious about your health, with more vigour. To do this requires a sound understanding of what we mean by health and a healthy lifestyle so that every choice we make about any activity we undertake is one which will impact positively on our health.

The World Health Organisation, WHO, defined health as a "state of complete physical, mental and social well-being and not merely the absence of disease or infirmity." Clearly this definition recognizes some common dimensions of health:

- Physical
- Mental
- Emotional
- Intellectual
- Spiritual
- Social

Additionally, there are factors, over which we may have no control, such as our genetic disposition. There are environmental factors such as industrial pollution over which, individually, we have little or no control. However, we have full control over some factors which impact on our health. These include our choice of food, supplements, drinks, as well as the quantity and quality of exercise and rest. We have further responsibility for our health in making decisions on the use of medical and illegal drugs and alcohol.

Someone once said that who you are may be revealed by what you eat. I want to add that it is not just what you eat but how you eat it, what you drink with what you eat and how you work out what you eat and drink. Do you eat without thinking about the effect of your food choice on your body? Do you make wise eating choices knowing what is good and what is not? Do you eat with constraint or do you eat with wild abandon? Do you imbibe sweetened carbonated drinks or fruit drinks? Do you exercise moderately at least three times per week? Do you use or abuse drugs and alcohol?

The state of your health is partially in your control. One has to have balance in making healthy choices. It is true that most of our foods today are so highly refined or processed that we have taken the living nutritional value out of them. I was not the most nutritionally conscious person before nor am I a stickler for healthy eating after that unfortunate incident in my life. But…I do strive to make wise choices. The keyword here is: strive. On many occasions past, the lure of the aromatic temptation of fast foods or spicy local delicacies was too great to resist.

Despite being brought up on many foods that are now considered bad for us, I learnt along the way about making healthy food choices: colourful foods, fibre-filled foods, less oil, less sugar and the list goes on. Being unable to eat for so many months back in 2013, I also learnt a good lesson in balance. Life is short and unpredictable. It is meant to be enjoyed and lived to the fullest, in happiness. Food, good food is part of that enjoyment. This is translated simply to mean: eat well as far as possible but eat what you like sometimes, when the need for it is urgent or overpowering.

As for drinking, it ought to be enjoyable too but more importantly we drink for hydration. Are you making choices which satisfy your body's needs so that you do not become thirsty? Or are you selecting drinks that leave your body craving for hydration? To maintain this balance I mentioned, are you tipping the scale with sufficient physical activity based on your individual requirements? Or are you more comfortable not indulging in any form of exercise? Let us now examine each of these in some more detail as we explore the physical dimension of health.

Healthy Food Choices

One of the important health choices we can make is in our diet; the foods we eat ought to be carefully selected and blended so as to create the optimum conditions for health and wellness. When we eat a balanced diet, filled with fresh foods, then we pave the way for health and reduce the odds of ill-health. At the cellular level our bodies are able to send the correct messages for growth and repair. To maintain a body with a high immune system, we need to consume foods that are fresh and healthy. These foods should be produced in such a manner as to provide a sufficiently high level of nutrients with a correspondingly low level of toxins such as fertilizers and other environmental toxins. Ideally a diet ought to cater to your personal taste, metabolism, individual needs and availability of ingredients.

What works for one individual may not work for another. Our nutrient requirements and our bodies' ability to assimilate nutrients from different foods are highly personalised. I must emphasize that priority must be placed on personal responsibility for health. However, it is possible to have a generalized program for healthy eating which may be adjusted to suit individual needs. We all need to eat from the following main food groups – fresh fruits and vegetables; fish, meat products and eggs or soy products for vegans; peas and beans; whole grain or high fiber cereals; ground provisions; and milk and milk products or substitutes.

The ratio of fresh fruit and vegetables ought to be higher than our carbohydrate intake: aim for about six servings of the former per day. Our meat intake could be less than fruits and vegetables but still higher than carbohydrates. Carbohydrate intake could be approximately three servings per day or less; again it depends on your personal metabolism and digestion. In addition to what you eat, there are some things you ought to eliminate or minimize in your diet. These include caffeine in any form, refined sugars and flour and any products that contain artificial colourings, preservatives, hormones and antibiotics.

Prior to 2013, I ate pretty much anything I felt like eating. For most of my life I was always conscious of what, when and how much I ate. My weakness is dessert and by dessert I mean the decadent types, not the fresh fruit type. I love cakes and pastries. Ah a gooey, freshly made cinnamon bun, the aroma of which fills the air as it is baking, never failed to bring me to that point of weakness where I had to have at least one as it came out of the oven. Knowing my soft spot for sacchariferous snacks, I would eat less savory delights ensuring that I had room to consume those delectable desserts.

Thankfully, I have learned to curb my yen for such sweetness. Refined sugar has been referred to as the fertiliser for cancer cells –feeding off sugar, cancer cells grow at an exponential rate, rapidly becoming difficult to control. This piece of information is enough to help me decrease the amount of sugar I include in my diet. What is your weakness? Do you make an effort to keep your diet healthy yet stimulating enough to sustain?

I tried regularly to eat vegetables especially the cruciferous ones such as broccoli and cauliflower and the dark green ones such as spinach. I used to eat meats such as poultry, beef and lamb as well as seafood, my favourite being shrimp. Only when I crossed the age of forty did I make a concerted effort to include whole grain foods in my diet.

My reason for trying to eat healthily was not the best. I was concerned about my weight for most of my life. Not that I was overweight but I wanted to maintain what I considered an optimum weight. That optimum was partly based on the traditional height to weight and body mass index figures but actually, it was mostly determined by how I felt and how my clothes fit.

Beyond a certain maximum I felt lethargic. I had trouble with flexibility. My joints would be achy and I suffered with general malaise. Then there was the problem with self-esteem. If my clothes did not look the way I wanted them to look, then I would be uncomfortable and immediately change my diet in an effort to get back to my optimum weight. The struggle was ongoing.

As I grew older, the optimum and the esteem changed. I became more comfortable with more weight gradually. Still, I would be conscious of my food choices in terms of amount, quality and times of consumption.

Prior to the incident, my weight had peaked! I felt great though because I was also physically active, running for about an hour at least three times per week as well as doing strenuous yard work occasionally. I may have been more accepting of this maximum because with maturity came self-confidence and acceptance.

During the recuperation time after the incident when I could not eat solids, my diet was easy to control. I could not eat; even if I tried it was impossible. My jaws were wired together. I could get nothing but fluids past my teeth which remained shut together. On occasion, it was frustrating. Several times I remembered my jaws were wired only as I was about to pop grapes eagerly into my mouth. There was even a time when a friend bought me an ice cream cone and I realized that I needed to have a straw just as I was about to taste it. Frustration!

Those times aside, my diet was, as I said, easy to control. I would have cream of wheat cereal for breakfast every morning along with a cup of tea or juice depending on my mood. Mid-morning I would have a fruit smoothie or an Ensure (or occasionally an ice cream). Lunch would consist of a watery soup made of chicken, peas, carrots and any other available vegetables along with garlic and onions and seasonings. This would, of course, have to be blended. Dinner was never a big deal for me. On most nights I would be satisfied with a cup of warm Milo.

Controlling my diet was one factor in the lack of weight gain at that time. Another factor would have been that my body was still in recovery mode. I had lost a significant amount of blood and there was a lot of physical injury. All of my internal resources were being directed toward physical healing. As mentioned previously, tissue, muscles, nerves and bone were seriously damaged. The body was in a state of repair and, along with the limited diet, there would have been negligible amounts of nutrient intake being converted into storage.

All factors taken into consideration, I recognized that the patterns of paying attention to my diet over the years contributed to the relatively remarkable pace of recovery. It is vital, then, to educate yourself about healthy eating choices, making sure to include lots of vegetables and fruits, colourful foods and to have a good balance of carbohydrates, fats proteins, vitamins and minerals as well as fibre.

It is not the aim of this book to provide a guide to healthy eating but rather to promote awareness of the need to be conscious of the food choices you make. Making proper food choices assists in overall well-being. However, with the high degree of refining, over-processing and use of fertilizers, pesticides, herbicides, hormones, additives and preservatives ubiquitous in the agricultural sector, even the best planned meals may not be providing us with adequate nutrients.

SUPPLEMENTS

If our food is no longer the ideal source of nutrition, then what are we to do? How do we maintain the levels of nutrients our bodies require to function daily? In times of health challenges, the problem becomes more pronounced. The body calls for more and more consistently valuable nutrients. Faced with the difficulty of acquiring nutrients when I was not eating and being acutely aware of the small quantities I was consuming, knowing that I was not getting sufficient nutrients, I consulted my doctors about supplementing my diet. The response was lukewarm. But having been an amateur runner, being weight-conscious and reading a lot about nutrition and diet, I felt differently. I began to supplement my diet in an effort to be proactive and to take responsibility for my health.

Many persons take at least one dietary supplement per day. Dietary supplements include:

- vitamins
- minerals

- herbals and botanicals which provide phytonutrients
- amino acids
- enzymes.

Do you supplement your diet and, if you do, how do you take your supplements? Do you take them regularly, at the same time every day? Do you take them when you remember? Do you take them when you experience symptoms of ill health? Are they taken once a day, twice or three times per day? Are you consistent, taking them every day? Do you stay away from them on weekends? Do you use tablets, capsules, powders, drinks or energy bars? These are all ways that people do actually take their supplements. I try to be consistent with the intake of a daily multivitamin.

When my body was depleted during recuperation from the gunshot wound and reconstructive surgery, I needed to take a general supplement and selected one which provided a wide range of vitamins, minerals and phytonutrients. I had to dissolve the multivitamin in order to consume it. Being rich in phytonutrients (nutrients from plants), the taste was not very pleasant. However the effect on my body was noticeable. When I was consistent with the doses, I was able to endure the days. When I got complacent with the doses, my body would break down and the day would leave me drained of energy, as the liquid diet was not adequate by itself.

Additionally, the loss of bone mass from my jaw and then from my hip after the hip graft (as outlined in my book, From Lion to Lamb) suggested that a calcium supplement was vital. Calcium supplements are best absorbed by the body when complemented by Magnesium and vitamin D, so I took one that provided all three together. Having a history of vague joint problems, I included glucosamine and omega-3. A vitamin B complex capsule was added, as I had been diagnosed with a vitamin B deficiency even before the incident.

In addition to these, I started taking antioxidants and a scavenger for lead. I was fearful of the presence of lead in my body owing to the possible presence of bullet shrapnel. Most was removed but there was no guarantee that all was taken out.

I must add that these supplements were taken at different times so as to preclude interactions which may decrease their potency or cause adverse reactions. Again, while the purpose of this book is not to instruct as to what, if any, supplements you need to take, I want to emphasize the importance of being responsible for your health. Your doctors know a lot but no one is infallible. Read, discuss with those who are more informed than you and analyse before deciding on your course of action with respect to supplements. As further encouragement, one of my doctors recently told me that my recovery was amongst the best, even including those treated in more developed countries.

The recommended drink for oral supplements is water. Caffeinated drinks and hot drinks such as coffee, tea or carbonated drinks apparently interfere with the rate and level of absorption of supplements, just as they are purported to do with oral medications. Research has linked the use of grapefruit juice with increasing the potency of certain medications. It is widely acknowledged and scientifically proven that alcohol use is not appropriate with medication. The use of these two types of drinks with supplements ought to be limited or not at all, to err on the side of caution. Thus, while supplementation may be important, it appears that the liquid used to wash it down has to be carefully considered.

HYDRATION

As was suggested in the last section, equally important as what is eaten and the supplements taken, are the liquids we drink. I drank a lot during recuperation after the shooting injury. In fact that was all I could do. Even though I drank the occasional milkshake, loaded with sugary goodness, I tried to keep it to a minimum. My greatest sacrifice after 2013 was limiting sugar and soda intake.

One particular carbonated beverage was my number one drink of choice for many years. I was addicted to it. I would have at least one every day, at breakfast time. When my mouth was under threat after the incident, I made the conscious decision to break the habit. Now, on the very rare occasion, when I feel listless, I may reach for one.

Generally the high sugar content of many carbonated drinks is undesirable: the use of such drinks promotes unhealthy choices ultimately contributing to diabetes, obesity and hyperactivity. In addition, the acid content of some of these drinks may be linked to loss in bone density and tooth erosion. The carbon dioxide content leaves the consumer feeling bloated.

Additionally, I carefully regulated my consumption of fruit juices. First, many fruit juices are loaded with added sugar. Second, I had noticed a spike in pain, swelling and fever in my joints upon drinking fruit juices, particularly citrus drinks. Consequently this choice of beverage was usually a last resort for me. This, I must note, is an individual reaction. Careful attention to and analysis of your body's responses are important in determining the extent to which different types of food and drinks are included in your diet.

Three drinks became more important to me during the recovery period: water, coconut water and green tea. As I consider myself a runner, the importance of hydration was and is always imminent in my mind. As tasteless as it is colourless, water may not be appealing, particularly to those who have a sweet tooth. However given that most of the planet and most of our bodies are made up of those vital, v-shaped molecules of H_2O, it may be in our best interest to make the sacrifice of taste over health benefits.

This is not the forum for a detailed account of the biochemical goodness of water but briefly, water replenishes what we lose during the course of a day through perspiration, tears and excretion. It is important to help in keeping the balance in and diluting toxins which pass through our kidneys and liver. Blood plasma has a high water concentration as does saliva, digestive juices and ocular cells. It prevents cells and cell membranes from becoming flaccid.

Although there is a high metabolic water requirement, water alone is insufficient for hydration. Hydration includes intake of essential electrolytes. Simply, electrolytes are a variety of salts or ions needed in the body, the most commonly known being sodium, potassium and bicarbonate ions. Electrolytes play a vital part in regulating the balance of fluids in the body as well as maintaining proper functioning of the nervous system, the heart, the kidneys and muscular system and regulating the pH or acidity of blood.

Water does not contain these electrolytes. Coconut water, however, does contain electrolytes. In fact coconut water is described as an isotonic beverage, meaning that its concentration of electrolytes is similar to our body's plasma. More than that coconut water is also said to contain vitamins, trace elements and enzymes all of which contribute to better cell functioning.

Green tea is another powerful drink. It contains all the benefits of regular black tea but without the caffeine. It is supposed to be chock full of antioxidants, useful molecules to combat free radicals in our bodies which promote aging. The free radicals find themselves in our systems through several methods including excessive sun exposure and exercise. A host of vitamins, enzymes and other phytonutrients combine in this powerhouse of a drink.

Hydration contributes to having healthy neural pathways. This means that we are able to process information better, to send signals from the brain faster and more effectively and generally to function at a higher level than if we are not properly hydrated. A balanced diet, well supplemented, along with sufficient water and electrolytes contribute to making us well poised for building resilience. However, sometimes our bodies become oversaturated and the need arises to abstain or fast from certain elements in our diets.

FASTING

Not having grown up with a regular practice of fasting, it took a while for me to build it into my diet. Over the years I tried to fast occasionally. But after the incident, fasting became a regular part of my routine. There are multiple purported benefits of fasting: weight loss, particularly stomach fat; reduced possibility of developing type II diabetes; reduced oxidative stress and; physical and spiritual cleansing. These multiple advantages, coupled with potential neuropathic benefits play a significant role in equipping the body to deal with the rigors of stress and adversity. Bear in mind that I am not a medical expert. It is recommended that you consult a medical doctor before beginning any fasting practice, especially if you are very young, old or have a particular health problem.

Practicing fasting has become a fixture in my diet. I do it before an auspicious time in my calendar such as during the Lenten season or before speaking engagements. I research the types of fasting before actually indulging in the practice. The heightened sense of awareness is heady and compelling. My most memorable and valued fasting session was carried out in 2015 when I attended a preaching seminar while fasting. I had fasted for four days before the seminar and was still fasting on the actual day. The result was that I functioned at a transcendental level. I left the seminar with a sense of peaceful fulfillment and rejuventation, similar to the feeling resulting from a proper rest.

Rest

For most of us getting enough sleep or rather restful sleep presents a problem. Sometimes we look at television or use the computer until late at night. Our brain becomes super stimulated and rest does not come easily at that time. Or sometimes we are anxious and worried for a variety of reasons. We wonder about the state of our financial affairs, our children and their future or their whereabouts or even about what is happening at an international level in terms of the economy or the increasing violence. Such issues are given mental prominence which precludes sleep.

Unfortunately our humanity requires us to get a certain minimum number of hours of sleep or rest to recharge. On the seventh day, after creating the world, God rested. This alone speaks volumes about the importance of rest in any undertaking, as massive as world creation or as insignificant as conducting daily chores. If you are serious about making healthy choices then you cannot or ought not to neglect getting sufficient rest. Sleep is not passive; the body is in an active state with wide ranging brain activity during sleep, perhaps more so than during waking times. The waveforms obtained from persons in sleep are surprisingly varied with respect to brain waves, eye movement and muscle tension.

Providing the right conditions are met, sleep promotes self-healing during the time when the body is unconscious with a reduced response to external stimuli. During this time different parts of the brain are stimulated whilst other parts remain dormant. Sleep patterns may be divided into four stages followed by a rapid eye movement (REM) phase. As the body begins to relax the wave forms of the wakeful mind begin to get slower and to be more consistent in their pattern than during full wakefulness. This aspect of sleep, just before stage 1, appears to be the most beneficial from a physiological standpoint.

Following this, the body begins to shift into stages 1 and 2 of sleep. During this time the brain waves get even slower and there is a subtle change from stage 1 to stage 2 of sleep. The sleeper can be easily awakened from rest at this time. As sleep continues the sleeper shifts into stage 3 with even slower waves and eventually into stage 4. These stages are what we call "deep sleep". A person prematurely awakened during these stages will be confused and befuddled. The brain waves generated during stages 3 and 4 are very different from those derived when awake.

Following stage 4 is the REM stage of sleep. The brain is very active and waveforms very much like those during wakefulness are produced. This stage is characterized by the eyes moving or darting in all directions very rapidly and by a simultaneous loss of muscle tone reminiscent of being paralyzed- the heart and other essential muscles remain functioning. Dreams are vivid and realistic during this phase.

Sleep starts at stage 1 then moves through the other stages to REM for ninety minute cycles during the course of the night. At every cycle the length of REM increases.

The endocrine system releases several hormones during sleep; one of particular importance is the growth hormone responsible in part for repair in the body. Renal functions and alimentary activity are reduced during this time. Interestingly those who undergo chronic sleep loss will find themselves in a situation where cortisol (stress hormone) levels do not decrease in the manner they should under normal sleeping conditions. Instead the levels are increased and could promote insulin resistance, which in turn could predispose one to diabetes and obesity.

For those who are conscious about calorie intake, this may peak your interest: sleep and food are intimately related. The levels of hormones which regulate appetite have been found to be linked with sleep deprivation. The less you sleep the more calories your body requires to be satiated. Some effects of lack of sleep on body functions include:

- possibly higher calorie requirements owing to lower levels of the hormone(leptin) present in fat cells that suppresses appetite;
- an increased desire for high carbohydrate foods owing to increased production of a peptide called gherlin which stimulates appetite and;
- reduced glucose tolerance.

In my own case, during the recuperation phase after being shot and undergoing reconstructive and plastic surgery, recuperation involved a lot of sleeping, both natural and medically induced. This was necessary for restorative and repair work to be conducted during these so called dormant times. We have now much more research and scientific evidence to show that sleep is not passive but indeed an active and vital process for our well- being. The process of bouncing back effectively from any setback is greatly enhanced by incorporating sufficient rest and sleep in your daily routine. In fact, rest days improve the ability to bounce back better, as can be attested to by anyone who is aware of or indulges in fitness or training programmes.

Regular Exercise

People exercise for different reasons: some are motivated to lose weight; some do it because it was recommended by their doctor; others do it professionally; still others do it because it makes them feel good. I exercise regularly for three reasons:

1. To lose weight or maintain weight depending on my status at the time
2. To aspire to become fit and healthy
3. To compete for medals

Prior to 2013, I ran at least three times per week for a half an hour to an hour on afternoons. In 2013, as described in my book From Lion to Lamb, I was shot during an attempted robbery. Neither my car nor possessions were lost but I lost over a year of my life (it could have been my life itself) undergoing surgery and recuperation.

I am convinced that recuperation was faster than expected by the doctors because of the level of my physical fitness among other factors. I recall, even while at the hospital, as soon as I began walking again, I started to do laps, walking slowly of course, from my bed to the end of the ward, approximately twenty feet in length. At first, I could only make it halfway to the door before having to return to my bed. I gradually increased that to at least three or four laps.

I even lifted water bottles as weights on occasion, as I tried to keep my muscles active! I regularly and faithfully did the exercises recommended by the hospital's physiotherapist. I was limited by the level of nutrition I was receiving and by the wide assortment of drugs administered to me – from painkillers, to antibiotics and antidepressants as well as antihistamines. The idea is that you need to incorporate exercise into your daily routine, even if it is just to use the stairs more often, for instance.

Now almost four years after the incident, I am trying to regain some level of fitness. I am doing this because I started regaining some of the thirty pounds I had lost. It also helps me mentally as I work out alone; this gives me time to think while I run or walk. My mind is clearer after running and I experience bouts of euphoria after an especially good run. By getting back into a routine, I feel more in control of my life. I sleep better and I have more energy and feel fitter. You can choose your favorite workout routine to address health and fitness; it could be walking, running, swimming, dancing, cycling, Zumba or any of your favorite sports!

My reasons for exercising are universal reasons; they are not limited to running or walking. But, there are even more benefits associated with exercise. Research has shown exercise to be linked to a plethora of health benefits. It must be noted that this refers to regular and sustained efforts at physical activities, not a sporadic attempt without commitment to the cause. Some of the desirable outcomes associated with exercise are listed below.

Regular exercise is linked to:

- a deceleration of premature aging manifested by an extension of the average functional lifespan
- an overall reduction in cardiovascular risk including heart disease, stroke and metabolic syndrome as a result of increased production of the healthy HDLs (high density lipoproteins) and decreased level of unhealthy triglycerides
- strengthening of bones owing to positive stress on the bones as a result of weight bearing exercises and the use of resistance machines. It may even encourage bone growth thereby combating osteoporosis

- a more conditioned muscular system which improves body alignment and affords better protection for the internal organs. This also assists in controlling type II diabetes : as the strength and size of muscles increase, the use of glucose or sugars in the body becomes more efficient, which aids in the control of type II diabetes
- preventing or combatting arthritis
- weight control by burning of calories

These possible outcomes of exercise are all physiological benefits. There are also psychological advantages associated with **consistent** physical activity. Regular exercise is linked to improved cognitive function. Exercise seems to promote neurogenesis or the creation of new neurons in the hippocampus, that part of the brain which is responsible for memory and learning. (Neurons are cells in the brain that transmit information by electrical and chemical signals).

Physical activity assists in combatting depression and in mood enhancement. Exercise stimulates the production of "feel good" chemicals or hormones in the body and is simply fun. A short, incomplete list of these hormones and/or neurotransmitters is given below:

- **Endorphins** released cause you to feel exhilarated and reduce the effects of pain, creating a feeling commonly referred to as the 'runner's high'
- **Dopamine** is the hormone responsible for pleasure: working out is one way of increasing dopamine levels in the body
- Higher levels of **serotonin** in the body, produced as a result of exercise, work synergistically with endorphins to increase happiness and restful sleep
- **Norepinephrine** (noradrenalin) and **epinephrine** (adrenalin) work together in the "fight or flight" mechanism in the body; together they increase: heart rate; release of glucose from energy stores; and blood flow to muscles

There are three main categories of exercise: aerobic or cardiovascular training; strength or resistance training; and flexibility training. Particularly as we get older, it becomes increasingly important that we start, or become more committed to an exercise programme which caters to each of these categories. Of course, the earlier we begin the greater will be the health payoffs.

Aerobic or cardiovascular training immediately brings to my mind a marathon runner: this type of training builds endurance and increases the heart rate while strengthening the heart. Typical exercises would be walking, jogging, running, swimming or hiking. The rate or intensity of your workout would depend on where you are at on the fitness scale: the less fit you are the slower your rate or lower the intensity of your workout; approximately thirty minutes per day for at least three times per week is recommended.

Strength or resistance training conjures images of a muscular individual with a streamlined and well-oiled body. The use of body weight or isometrics or weight lifting or even resistance machines helps to develop the strength and size of muscles. This results in added stability of the skeletal structure as well as more efficient use of glucose stores. Some persons, particularly women and more so in the past, believed that they would develop unwanted muscles if they did strength training. Unless you are taking steroids and high protein supplements, it is unlikely that you will develop the sculpted look of a body builder.

Flexibility training and yoga are almost synonymous. As we grow older our muscles and joints become more rigid; less flexible. To combat this, stretching exercises are highly recommended along with several nutritional supplements as already mentioned. Yoga, Tai Chi and other stretching exercise classes are beneficial to any age group and any gender.

Before beginning any programme though, persons over forty years old or with a health challenge, need to consult a physician. Additionally, any programme adopted must be part of the selected lifestyle choices made for good health: this implies avoiding alcohol, smoking and other drugs, proper nutrition, positive thinking, use of recommended supplements and medications, rest and consciousness of your stress levels in different situations so that you may be able to bring down those levels as necessary.

A word of caution is necessary: excessive exercising is undesirable as it places undue oxidative stress on the body with increased levels of undesirable free radicals and it compromises the immune system. The addictive effect of the endorphins released during exercise is similar to the effect produced by opiates such as morphine.

Are you sufficiently stimulated by exercise and its multiple health benefits to become or to remain committed to exercise?

Committing to the principles of good health, a balanced diet, supplementation, proper hydration, fasting, rest and exercise is preparation for unexpected times of difficulty. These practices serve the body well making good times better and increase physical capacity to strive and thrive during and after bad times.

Develop Physical Stamina Exercises

1. Educate yourself on healthy eating practices.
2. Realistically assess your lifestyle: are you making healthy choices?
3. Eat so that you incorporate sufficient carbohydrates, proteins, fats and fiber in adequate proportions.
4. Eat colourful foods.
5. Try to eliminate excesses in the consumption of refined sugar and flour. Plan to reduce use of sugar to sweeten tea either gradually by cutting back to one teaspoon per cup or abruptly by using none at all. Limit intake of bread, roti, cakes and pastries. If you must have these, then it is best to consume them earlier in the day.
6. Drink water and coconut water regularly throughout the day. Start each morning with at least one cup of water before consuming anything else.

7. Consult with a medical professional and do your own research to determine the need for supplements and fasting.

8. Incorporate partial fasting into your routine. You may start gradually for example by eating your last meal for the day at an earlier time and having the first meal of the next day at least one hour later than usual. Again if you have a health challenge you need to consult with a professional before any fasting.

9. Eliminate distractions from your bedroom to ensure proper rest: take off or remove the television, avoid using the computer just before going to bed and put up dark curtains or blinds to eliminate external lights.

10. Begin some form of physical activity or commit to resuming one.

11. Sign up for a fun run or walk such as a 5K or get an exercise buddy for accountability.

Key Learning Points

1. Repast or fast and boost. Eat healthy meals based on correct proportions of carbohydrates, fats, proteins and fiber. Abstain from eating for selected periods under medical supervision or guidance. Supplement your diet after careful discussion with a professional, research and analysis.

2. Hydrate to invigorate.

3. Sleep and rest to be your best.

4. Be active: include regular exercise in your regime. Find activities that are a good fit for you; do what stimulates you and has you wanting to get up in the morning. It may be running, walking, cycling, Zumba, high intensity interval training (HIIT) or swimming.

Step 5

SEEK SUPPORT

"Cultivate relationships;
strengthen support networks and
fast track recovery."

O NE OF THE attractions of network marketing and franchises is the support which is provided. Both types of businesses put a lot of effort into training, providing tools and having a network of other persons, who can offer advice, lend a helping hand or an attentive ear. If you are willing to learn and willing to work with others then your business will boom. Similarly in any life situation, good or bad, support is of paramount importance.

Scientific literature identifies social support as help accessed through relationships with other individuals, groups, or within the community. It describes support as being two dimensional, consisting of a structural dimension and a functional dimension. Structure in this sense, includes the number of relationships as well as how regularly contact is established among the parties. Functional support consists of such emotions such as love and empathy as well as practical assistance, which involves the giving of time or money or expertise.

Further, the literature suggests that while both types of support are important, functional support is more closely linked as a predictor of good health. Whether functional or structural, support is suggested to be as critical to life expectancy as obesity, cigarette smoking, hypertension and one's level of physical fitness. It must be noted that while most references to support discuss it as a positive factor for good health, sometimes support may in fact have negative consequences. This plays out, for example, in the case of job loss when the feeling of having let down the family or support network could lead to depression and other negative consequences.

It seems that the extent to which support impacts upon good health and resilience is a complex interplay of several factors, inclusive of environmental and genetic factors. It appears to be optimally beneficial if it is in alignment with the specific needs and personalities of both the supporter and the one being supported as well as if it fits into the imperatives of need.

In this context, support may be classified into four main, sometimes overlapping categories:

- physical
- emotional
- mental
- spiritual.

Essentially, by definition, support is that which bears the burden of the weight of something; it is the ability of something to sustain effort especially during or when under pressure. The word brings to mind actual or virtual scaffolding which keeps various parts together as a whole. The goal of having support is to be able to transition more smoothly and quickly from a state of adversity to a state of prosperity. For example, on losing his or her job, having good support can enable an individual to cope with the loss, to better manage symptoms associated with the loss, including depression and other related problems and to be motivated to begin the search for an alternative income source.

The amazing fact of support is that both the giver and receiver benefit. So by supporting others, you accrue benefits for yourself. While this is not the noblest reason for being supportive, it does not detract from the need for support which we all have at different times in our lives. Let us examine the different forms of support we may need to seek out when striving to thrive.

PHYSICAL SUPPORT

Physical support could be provided in a few ways. For example it could mean standing side by side with someone or holding that person's hand in a doctor's office as they are about to receive a vaccination shot. Alternatively, it could mean erecting a wooden or metal structure around which a building is constructed, or which may be used to do repairs or for painting. It could even be the posts or fence or structure built to facilitate the growth of a vine such as a grape vine.

When related to human beings, physical support could mean lending or giving someone cash when they are in financial difficulty. It could mean providing groceries, a cooked meal or clothing to those in need. It could mean being present or doing something to ease the person's burden, such as providing transport or books or a bed for a good night's rest. Let me share an example of physical support with you from my personal experience.

After my lower jaw was fractured in 2013 and after undergoing surgery, my upper and lower jaws ought to have been wired together. However, the doctors at the time felt it was in my best interest not to do this as there was still a substantial amount of shrapnel left embedded in my jaws and surrounding tissues. It was their view that not wiring immediately would pre-empt the onset of secondary infections. Additionally they felt the jaw was too unstable to be able to sustain being wired.

Three weeks later, after many cleaning procedures and debridement, another doctor recommended that the jaws ought to be wired before any further damage was caused owing to the delay in wiring. It is usual practice that jaws should be wired shut immediately after being broken, to maintain their original shape. In my case, two main factors worked against me, which resulted in the internal collapse and calcification of my lower jaw. One factor was that the jaw had been left unwired for too long after the injury and the other factor was related to removing part of the jaw.

The reality was that the shape of the jaw had become distorted because its bone had started to heal in a very awkward direction; the teeth of the upper and lower jaws could not be properly aligned. Consequently, the oral maxillofacial surgeon at the hospital was confronted with the task of having to re-break the jaw before doing the wiring. A lack of support for the broken jaw, in its time of excessive stress, caused it to become deformed and to collapse inwardly.

In such stressful times as when a loved one or a job is lost, or when a diagnosis of ill health is received, or when a relationship has ended or even when a bad examination result is obtained, support is critical. Without support the person experiencing stress may begin to cave in under the burden of coping alone. Indeed, physical support plays an important part in the healing process. While physical support alone is good, emotional, mental and spiritual types of support are also key elements in recovery because we are not one-dimensional beings.

EMOTIONAL SUPPORT

Emotional support takes support to a higher level. No type of support is more important than the other. I suggest that they are equally weighted although there may be disagreement with this statement. I have observed that the personality and mindset of the individual undergoing the stress plays an important part in determining the weighting of each type of support.

For example, by nature I am an introvert. I used to consider myself fiercely independent and loved to do things for and by myself and to spend a lot of time by myself. The type of support I need is to have at least one person willing to listen to my problem; one person who empathizes with me. I may not need too much financial support. I may not require anyone to do anything for me (unless I really was physically unable to do things for myself). I do however thrive on emotional support.

When my dad was ill, one of my aunts felt it was unnecessary for both my mother and me to be simultaneously present with him all the time. She, being more pragmatic than we, felt that we needed to have a shift system for staying with him to preclude burning out at the same time. I was very upset with her for not wanting me to spend as much time as I could with my father. For me being present with him, even if I fell asleep briefly, was important. I felt that he would derive a sense of security knowing that I would be there for him if he needed anything at any time. I knew that staying would optimize the time I had left with him.

The point is that my aunt had her own ideas about support, my father must have had his own support ideals and I too had my own perspective. The three perspectives may have been different with some validity associated with each. She placed great emphasis on getting things done. I placed great emphasis on my father's emotional well-being although I balanced it out with getting things done. My dad appeared to be grateful for all the support.

So coming back to emotional support, what does it really mean? It means having someone around you to be **empathetic**. It means being able to discuss or just talk about what you are going through, how you are feeling with someone else. It means knowing that the listening ear will not judge you or dismiss your feelings as unimportant. Emotional support could overlap with physical presence; knowing that someone else is in the same room or house with you is a comfort in and of itself. You do not even have to talk with or see the other person.

My students sent many notes, letters, cards and gifts for me after the incident. Without ever being able to visit, they became a source of emotional support. It was soul-stirring whenever I read their words. I was so overcome with emotion by the love which leapt out of their writings that I knew I could not allow myself to fall into the trap of self-pity. I had to prove to these little ones that I was made of the kind of mettle I used to tell them **they** needed to develop.

Nine months after that life changing incident in my life, I began to have flash backs, nightmares and cold sweating, sometimes for no discernible reason. Sometimes it would be a thought, a statement, a person or a situation which would act as a trigger for an episode. An episode could be a flashback, a nightmare, wanting to scream aloud, tensing or becoming nauseated. There was no one with whom I wanted to share my thoughts. I remember one evening my mother and I were going to deliver some tickets for one of her friends. At no point in time did she realize we had to pass right where I had been shot.

For some noble reason I did not remind her. I reasoned with myself that it would be a form of therapy for me. As we approached the area, I started to cold sweat. I grasped the sides of the car seat with increasing force. I internally cringed when I saw the spot where I was transferred to the police vehicle, with blood pouring in a seemingly endless stream from my face. I felt the bile rise as we drew nearer to the spot where the incident actually occurred. I felt as though my whole body was rejecting the experience but I sat stoically as I battled to maintain my composure.

My mother was clueless. She just thought I wanted to be quiet. She could not have known the trauma I was going through; she could not have imagined the thoughts going through my mind. I did not want her to know. She was a major player in my new support framework. Her equilibrium had to be stable so that we could all re-achieve some sort of normalcy. I could not let her know the depths of despair in which I was dangerously wallowing.

The day I broke down in public, sobbing like a lost child in front of many strangers, I knew I had to seek support for my emotional and mental health. I opted for professional assistance, recognizing the extent to which this trauma had seeped into my psyche. Thankfully my doctor concurred and I was referred to the Psychiatric Clinic at the San Fernando General Hospital. There I was diagnosed, given a medical prescription and received counselling from a social worker.

The counselling was a vital part of my emotional healing. As a consequence of the counseling, I had someone with whom I could talk, someone who would listen without judging (or who at least would give the appearance of not judging), and someone who would not be too emotionally tied in with me but could still be empathetic. The combined treatment of drugs and counselling brought relief and helped me to change my perspective and approach to recovery. I was able to release negative emotions by confronting them. The memories were still there; the flashbacks would still occur but their frequency diminished and the debilitating effect they had on my emotional state began to wane.

The security of knowing my family was available if I needed them coupled with the professional help garnered through therapy provided the emotional support that is so vital to coping and recovering in difficult times. The reality is that life does go on after any type of obstacle arises. Physical and emotional support cushion potentially devastating effects of adversity but mental support is needed for forward movement.

MENTAL SUPPORT

Mental support and emotional support are linked but there are differences. Mental support or intellectual support brings the emotional relief of knowing that someone in your immediate circle has some intellectual value for you. It could mean that someone close to you is knowledgeable about income taxes, about the diagnosis you are facing, they may know the right people who could help you, they may know of job openings or may know of next steps you need to take in your situation or if they do not know, they are capable and willing to research it for you.

In my case, being isolated at the hospital, without a telephone, a laptop or kindle or any techie device and no internet access, my mental support was provided by family and friends. My brother questioned, probed and prodded until he was able to find out about the best possible treatment for me. My friends provided information about sick leave and extended leave.

Whatever the nature of your distress is, mental support has a role. If you are under examination stress, then your teacher or a well-informed peer will provide much needed support. If you are facing a critical diagnosis such as cancer or diabetes, then someone may provide research on the latest treatments or details about the nature of the disease. For someone who has lost his or her job, then knowledge of compensation plans and procedures would be needed; support, then, could mean providing a list of vacancies or alternative sources of income, it may even be providing contact information for others who may have the knowledge.

In the case of the loss of a loved one, a supporter may provide information on the procedures to be adopted in carrying out the final rites. They may provide information on what has to be done legally and who may be able to help. Following a relationship break up mental support may mean providing information for a much needed vacation, a getaway or it may be providing the name of a good counsellor, such as a social worker or a priest. Providing the name of a priest is classified as supporting mentally but going to the priest for advice and prayers translates into spiritual support.

SPIRITUAL SUPPORT

A priest or other religious leader may be associated with spiritual support which in turn is related to having strong faith. It means being able to place your hope on something that is unseen. For an increasing number of persons that unseen is referred to as the Universe. For many others it refers to God. A large percentage of people do not have faith in a greater being. Some of these people never change their outlook but some do.

When faced with a highly traumatic event many people, who never believed in a God, have emerged as believers. Then there are those who are unable to effectively bounce back because of a lack of good spiritual support. The research has shown that those with a strong spiritual backing are more resilient than those who are not spiritual.

I remember, after speaking at a session organized by the BOCAS

Literature Festival in South Trinidad in 2014, one lady asked me how I was able to recover from such a devastating blow as the one I had. She was curious as to how I thought someone who is an atheist would be able to draw the strength to emerge victorious through adversity from my story, which is faith based. My answer then was that I did not know because faith had been an integral part of my healing.

The research shows that there is a scientifically strong link between spirituality and recovery from physical, emotional or mental hurt. As a Christian, I strongly advocate my belief. For those who are not Christians, developing an inner conviction of a higher order of accountability may prove to be a vital link to optimism and resilience. There is a distinction between religion and spirituality. Religion is steeped in rituals and dogma whereas spirituality may be regarded as an inner conviction and persuasion which creates a protective shield against hurt.

A major player in the circuitry needed to successfully maneuver through the fog of despair or difficulty is support. This support may be expressed tangibly or imperceptibly through giving or doing things, by being empathetic, by being a source of information or by coming together in prayer and faith. Those who have strong connections are fortunate. They need only to continue nurturing those relationships that form their support network. Those without connections or with a weak framework of support need to begin cultivating rich relationships, bearing in mind that the research emphasizes quality not quantity of members in a network.

Seek Support Exercises

1. Call at least one person for the day.
2. Schedule and meet a friend or family member for coffee or lunch or to exercise or other activity.
3. Be nice to, smile and chat with someone new as you go about your daily routine.
4. Become an active member of a support or philanthropic group.

5. Spend time with or help someone who is also going through a difficult time.

6. Reach out for professional help if the burden of your affliction becomes too great to handle alone.

7. Turn to a spiritual leader for support.

Key Learning Points

1. Support is vital to help keep you from falling apart during a time of need.

2. Four main types of support are discussed: physical, emotional, mental and spiritual.

3. Build support networks during normal times to have a strong system in crisis times.

4. Reach out for support during crisis times, even if you did not previously cultivate relationships.

Step 6

FUNCTION IN FAITH

"Put pain in perspective;
be guided by infinite wisdom,
knowing that the final outcome
will be what it will be."

EVEN THE GREAT Albert Einstein, not believing in a personal God, believed in holding onto a transcendental outlook. He justified this view on many occasions. It was his belief that the world and its workings and orders and physical laws were too complex to be comprehended by our relatively small intellects. He compared human understanding of the mysteries of the universe to that of a child in a vast library; the child knows that the books are arranged in some order, that they must have been written by someone but he does not know by whom and that there are languages in the books that he does not understand. According to Einstein and others who share his beliefs, there is some greater force that controls the machinations of the universe; its greatness is too much for our finite minds to comprehend.

Einstein postulated three views of spirituality: one involved a spirituality developed from religious fear, one from social morality and one from a cosmic religious feeling. It was his view that the third, based on a cosmic religion, on an appreciation of the manifest beauty of order and physical laws, beyond reach of our mortal minds, was the most mature. He also argued that many atheists adopted the stance of disbelief in a God or gods, out of a perception of having thrown away the shackles of indoctrination perfectly placed during their formative years of religious instruction.

Beyond putting forward these ideas, he went on to describe in beautiful language the wonder of acknowledging and accepting a superior force behind the existence of our world and lamented for those who could not wrap their minds around such a concept, believing them to be backward in their thinking. He embraced the idea of believing in something which he could not see. He believed in having faith.

Having faith encompasses both religion and spirituality. Having faith means placing your beliefs into a realm beyond the comprehension of our intellect. It calls for an acknowledgement and acceptance of a force which is responsible for the complexities of this life, which we try to explain with physical laws, instinctively knowing these laws were laid down by a higher authority.

This faith is what resilient people call upon in their times of difficulty. Even atheists have been known to call on God in their most difficult times. History recalls many stories of converts, not necessarily to Christianity. Regardless, faith provides a lifeline to the spiritual, to the believers, onto which they may cling until they are safely out of the mire of adversity.

Whether you have lost a job, dream, loved one, home or limb, whether your financial situation is threatened, whether you are in a relationship crisis or facing a health situation, a strong spiritual outlook may prove to be a beacon to a harbour of peace and calm out of the turbulence in your life.

How does one turn to faith in a crisis? Is it not then easier to believe that there is no God? Is it not natural to consider this test to be confirmation that God does not exist or that you should not have faith? I ask instead, how does one not turn to faith in tough times? If there is no hope, how can one have optimism? Why should you try to navigate out of the turbulence? What is the purpose of your life, if there is not some higher order? From where does the strength come to deal with the sometimes mind-boggling trauma which may confront us?

This is a concept that is not fully understood, perhaps one which may never be grasped. Holding on to the belief that we are not in this universe alone but that there is a greater management involved is sometimes the only thing that makes sense when everything else is out of whack. For me faith was my sanity when my world came crashing down around me. I was able to let go of the enormity of all my problems, as I acknowledged that there was a higher purpose, not immediately comprehensible. The clarity of thought even at the lowest point in my personal trial was amazing to me even to this day.

I let go of constraining beliefs: that I had somehow done something to cause this to happen to me; that if there was a God, I would have emerged bullet-free; that my life no longer had any purpose and; that recovery would be limited and leave me a shadow of my former self. Of greater significance, I held on to beliefs that gave me freedom: that there was a greater being; that my injuries could have been worse; that my life's purpose would be revealed; that this incident would be the precipitating factor leading to my purpose; that recovery would be tremendous and leave me different but good.

The freedom I gained from having faith included being able to focus my strength into physical healing. Not having to deal with questioning why this happened or why God did not protect me, I was able to quiet my mind and divert negative energy into positive physical pathways. I used an age old method of focusing on God through scripture to draw on His greater strength whenever I had to undergo painful procedures. Even as I was being transported to the hospital immediately after the incident, I remained peaceful and calm.

I remember several months after the incident one of my former students met me. He started interviewing me about different aspects of that fateful night. He was really interested though in how I was able to deal with the pain from the time of being shot to the time I actually received painkillers. He did not seem too thrilled with my answer. I suspect he wanted a gory description of the blood, the bones and the bullets along with screaming and intense, unbearable pain.

I did not share such gory stories with him because, from the very instant I was shot, I shifted almost immediately into survival mode. Although the extent of my injury was beyond my imagination at that time, I did know that it was bad. The amount of blood pouring out of my face was testament to that. The screams from the driver did not help. However my brain went into overdrive. I knew I had to conserve my energy. I knew that I had to hold on to something that was not tangible. I knew that without faith the possibility of going insane was not…well, insane.

I drew from my childhood days of reciting the Lord's Prayer and John 3:16. I repeated the scripture verse so many times. I sang it when my memory began to be unreliable and I could not remember the words even as I tried to say it. I gave thanks to God for all the blessings I received that night and afterward.

The question now is how can anyone apply faith in a negative situation, especially someone who has not developed the practice of faith? One way is to displace your focus from yourself, without minimizing the extent of your own trauma. Look around at others who may be in similar situations or even worse situations than your own and know that you are not alone. Look at those who seem to be thriving and use that as an impetus that life will get better.

Another way to emerge out of a difficult situation is to remember that scientific laws are great predictors of behavior and action but there are always exceptions that cannot be explained by these laws. So even what may seem impossible to the world is possible through some higher source that our finite minds are incapable of processing. Have you ever heard of a confirmed cancer patient mysteriously coming into remission, sometimes for many years, sometimes with the diagnosis never returning?

Last year my mother went for a routine checkup to screen for the re-occurrence of any malignant growths after a mastectomy in 2012. The doctors found a significant growth in the left breast and made immediate arrangements to have it tested and removed. She turned to prayer in her despair and prayed desperately, holding onto the faith that it would not be there when she went back for the procedure. She was overcome with gratitude when she did return for testing: the doctors probed relentlessly without success. They found no trace of the lump. She has since gone back several times and there is still no lump to be found: faith or fiction?

Even if you do not think of yourself as a spiritual person and think that you do not have the faith about which I am writing, you do in fact have faith. Whatever we do is guided by a belief that it will work out. We do not undertake a project with the expectation that it will not succeed. We do what we do believing that we will see it to a successful completion. Many times along the way there may be obstacles. You may have to abandon one course of action in favour of another, but you keep hoping that in the end it will be alright.

This hope is a form of faith. I favour Godly faith, choosing to believe that there is a greater Mastermind behind the mysteries of the Universe but that does not mean I will discredit another's belief. What worked for me was acknowledging that there are two loci of control: one is internal; the other is external.

Internal control gives me the power to make choices where it is possible. For example, once I got to the point of acceptance of what had happened to me, I was able to choose to adopt a positive outlook that all would work out well. It would be different but I would survive and move forward. The alternative to that would have been to believe that my world would never be the same again and it would be worse than before with no chance of improvement.

External control remains out of my personal range. This means that although internal control allowed me to be optimistic, there were things that I could not avoid that may not be pleasant or that did not appear to be positive. For example, having my salary reduced by fifty percent after the first three months of sick leave, followed by having no salary after six months was out of my control. This was a legal matter. This was according to teaching service regulations. I could cry or complain but I could not change that situation.

It is important, especially in times of crisis situations, to recognize those things over which you have direct control and those things which are beyond your control. Recognizing the difference requires that you put faith into your choices, hoping, without seeing, that the sun will rise again and the rains will subside.

Develop Faith Exercises

1. Awake early on mornings to spend at least 15 -20 minutes in prayer and reading scripture.
2. Express gratitude for the blessings of life, health, family and friends for instance.
3. Commit at least one passage of scripture to memory daily. Recall scripture during difficult times as a source of strength and hope.
4. Listen to and sing hymns of praise and worship.
5. Spend time with companions who are steeped in faith.
6. Join a prayer group or scripture study group.
7. Worship with others.

KEY LEARNING POINTS

1. Faith is the belief in an unseen entity such as God, knowing that all will work according to His direction.
2. People who develop their faith tend to recover more readily and more completely than those without faith.
3. Recognize that there are factors within your control: know these and use them to your advantage.
4. Know that there are other factors outside of your control: attempting to manipulate these factors could lead to frustration and a loss of faith creating an obstacle to your progress.

Step 7

BE HUMBLE

"Reduce the decelerating effect of hurdles,
along the track of your life,
by practicing humility."

NTERWOVEN IN THE matrix of good character is humility. It stands out like golden strands against a dull background. Great leaders throughout history were people identified by their humility. Mahatma Gandhi, Mother Teresa and Martin Luther King Junior, who are internationally known, have achieved excellently and are associated with humility. Scattered across the landscape of humanity are many leaders of various walks in life whose trademark is humility.

In my own little world, I have observed that the people worthy of being considered successful live steeped in humility. By the average standard, success is measured by wealth or status. But true success runs deeper than either, alone or combined. True success is measured in terms of being able to lead a life of compassion, peace, love, forgiveness and humility. It does not mean that wealth and status automatically excludes you from the category of successful but it does mean that there is more to success than wealth and status.

What does it really mean to be humble? Apart from the obvious of not being proud, being humble could be interpreted in several ways. The word connotes the idea of subservience, of having a lower opinion of your own sense of self-importance. More than that, humility implies meekness. It may even apply to abasement. A humble person is more concerned about the welfare and feelings of others; knowing his worth, a humble person readily does what is necessary to help someone else.

I remember being asked a poignant question by one television personality on his morning programme back in 2014, just prior to the launch of From Lion to Lamb. I was asked if the entire experience of being severely injured and having to stay at the hospital for three weeks in a depleted condition was a humbling one. My respectful answer was, "Yes, it was!"

It was humbling at several levels. First I was subjected to being stripped in front of total strangers who were fighting to save my life. I have always been and remain a conservative person. Being completely undressed by and in front of strangers under normal circumstances would have been a concept completely out of my zone of comprehension. Given my state at that time, I had no choice and no feelings about the matter. Self- modesty was defenestrated.

But what was humbling too, was being dependent completely on others to survive. Initially, I had to be fed through a tube and was unable even to fill the tube for myself. I lay almost helpless for so many days, unable to speak, not wanting to awake at times. If someone did not fill the feed bag for me, there would be no feeding. If medication was not administered, I would be unable to fetch it for myself. If there were no pen and paper, communication with doctors, nurses or anyone for that matter would have been very limited.

Throughout my life, I always tried to have a neat appearance. Those weeks at the hospital would have been the only time in my life when it did not matter. I did not care too much about combing my hair or if my face was oily or that I had on no lipstick. I walked without concern through the corridors of the ward in a thin nightgown, uncombed hair, with bandages all over my face and a tube dangling from my nostrils. I did see people I knew but vaguely recognized them and they certainly did not know who I was until they recalled the incident or someone else pointed it out to them. Humbling? Yes!

Having lost my job (through retirement on medical grounds) and my car, my status in life changed. I now had to start rebuilding my financial stability from ground zero. It meant I had to be willing to no longer see myself as a teacher. I was now "retired", without a vehicle and with a permanently scarred face. Yes I had my life but what life? I had to be humble enough to begin to redefine who I was. I had to seek ways to avoid losing my house by not being able to meet mortgage payments.

What finally hit home was the fragility of life itself. All that seemed so important and urgent before paled to insignificance in the haze of that trauma. The only thing that really mattered was the greatness of God. To Him I submitted everything. All pain, all healing, all anger and all hurt. This was a key part of my eventual recovery. The main lesson out of this aspect of my story would be that humility removes the focus from self. Devotion to and faith in God serves to replace autonomy. Thinking of others and their needs diminishes the vastness of self.

When that single important shift of attention to humility begins to take place, then possibilities for moving forward begin. Action and inactivity dwell in opposite dimensions. Inactivity is fueled by self-pity and over-extended periods of being subjugated by personal trials. Grief in times of difficulty is inevitable; it is desirable up to a point. Grieving is healthy and necessary before acceptance takes place as we have seen in step 2. Acceptance brings with it a desire to re-start, a will to bounce back and to do it better than before. Humility brings acceptance of your current situation, no matter how bad it may be or seem.

However, sometimes the grieving cursor gets stuck on the keyboard of time. When that happens, inactivity sets in. Humility takes a back seat. Who has time for others when there is so much of one's own burdens with which to deal? How can one have empathy or be compassionate when wrapped in the cozy blanket of self-importance and grief? The road to recovery then becomes covered with a thick fog, through which it becomes difficult to navigate.

Without that fog, the way becomes clear. Action begins to take over and is powered by a willingness to be meek and to give up excessive thoughts of one's significance or rank or status. Progress becomes possible. Slowly the focus of attention shifts from self. Other people's perception of who we are or what happened to us begins to lose the claim we allowed it to have on our recovery.

In the midst of the greatest of traumas, it is possible to cut off the supply of fuel to feelings of despair and hopelessness by adopting a stance of humility. Yes, your condition may be dire, but by giving it too much attention, by watering and fertilizing it, you are not doing yourself any favours. Instead you will be in the same or a worse condition: inactivity will set in. The only thing that would seem to exist would be pain and hurt and no way out of it.

One of the keys to bouncing back is to adopt a stance of humility. Allow others to assist you. If you had never before accepted anything from anyone, do not let this time of difficulty be just like all other times. Accept assistance in humility. I remember never being able to accept anything from anyone, no matter how badly I may have needed their offering. At the lowest point in my life, humility stepped in to save my life; I was able to accept help in all different forms from family, friends and strangers.

A couple of years ago, there was one student whose family was in a crisis situation. Both parents were doing the best that they could at the time but they were still struggling financially. No matter how much effort was put into getting help for that family, they kept refusing to accept the help. They had known better times when the parents were able to support the family on their own but could no longer do so owing to circumstances over which they had no control. Having never had to ask for help, having a kind of pride which prevented them from wanting to let others know how bad their situation really was, they did not accept help.

Asking for and accepting help does not mean you do not want to help yourself. It just means that until such time as you could do for yourself, you will use the help extended in your direction. An attitude of meekness and humility allows us to accept help from others until we are capable of helping ourselves. A dose of wisdom is also needed. Wisdom reveals that without asking for help others may not be able to detect need. As well it reveals when it is right and imperative to accept help.

In the face of a critical situation, it is difficult to practice humility but that very thing is part of being humble. Doing what is most difficult is making humility real. In difficult times, more so than at other times, we are put to the test. Will you in the midst of your challenge be able to accept injustice without reacting in a grievous manner? Will you be able to accept the change in your status and treat it as a way of starting anew, possibly in a new direction? Will you be able to recognize that just as others make mistakes you also do the same, not necessarily the same mistakes but that you do make mistakes?

Will you be willing to do what it takes to maintain your dignity regardless of the external circumstances which may be threatening your life as you know it? Will you do whatever noble job or task you can do to be able to pay the bills and provide for you and your family?

The practical aspect of humility requires you to put aside thoughts of that on which man places so much emphasis: status. To bounce back better sometimes requires starting over, from a very low baseline. Do you have a skill or talent which may help you to earn an income? If you do, then you are lucky. Make that luck count. Use your skill or talent. Do not sit and wait for some windfall that may never come. Get up and start moving. Remember action is powered by meekness and brings with it the reward of positive forward movement.

As I mentioned earlier, I had to do a lot of starting over. I lost my job in the sense that it was recommended that I take retirement on medical grounds and I accepted it. After August 2013, my salary was completely cut. I began to live off my modest savings and would soon have to find a source of income to ensure payment of my mortgage.

Fortunately as a Chemistry teacher, although I now had restricted motion of my jaw, I could do private tuition. Luckily I was able to source several jobs that involved working from a computer, which could be done at home. My book and some of the resulting speaking engagements also became a source of income.

Another source of finance came from network marketing. Many persons are suspicious of network marketing but then we are always afraid of that which we do not know. I became a part of a networking system somewhat unwillingly. It has been a decision which I have not yet grown to regret. In fact it is one I now embrace and would recommend for others who may not know their skills or talents or who are at their wits end trying to find a business niche or start up idea. There are so many positives to being a part of a system that not only works but works for you! The point is that you need to be humble enough to open your mind to possibilities which you may not have even considered before.

Let me share this story on humility. One day I took my son to a former student's home for some assistance with an assignment he had to complete. The family was steeped in humility. The father had suffered an injury some years ago and was unable to work. The mother worked with a community maintenance company.

They downplayed their own importance and status, choosing instead to lift me up as a former teacher. There was nothing they did not want to do for me as I waited on my son. When we left that day, despite my protestations, the parents had packed a bag of vegetables that had been harvested from their own garden! What humility and love I experienced that day and... I learnt a valuable lesson. The lesson from that story was to practice humility by being kind, gentle and generous regardless of your current circumstance.

In April 2015 I attended a series of sermons at a church in South Trinidad. The preacher was visiting from the United Kingdom. His voice was calm and soothing. His message was simple but profound; as it turned out he was the personification of his message: authority with humility. What it meant is that you may have knowledge, skills, resources and status that others do not have; you have a duty to share with others for their edification but it must be done so as not to belittle them. Display authority with humility.

Sadly many people mistake humility for weakness. They fail to recognize that our number one priority is to be of service to others and to be humble in so doing. Even as the electricity went out on the first night of the service, the pastor persisted with his message. At the end I approached him, hoping to be able to say a few words to him. I was prepared to wait as long as I had to because so many others wanted to see him too. He turned to me immediately, as soon as he became aware of my presence, and I was able to get a few minutes to chat with him. As I departed he called me by my name as he bid me goodbye. A classic example of authority with humility!

Practicing Humility

We live in a world where humility appears to be an old fashioned quality. It is not valued in our highly commercial environment. In fact the virtue of humility seems to be best viewed from afar as a trait suitable for anyone but you. How can we practice humility in the action-packed, fast paced world in which we live? How can someone practice humility when their world is falling apart?

In good times or bad, we all seek to find meaning and significance in our lives. Many people indulge in this by diligently doing whatever it takes to keep making more money or getting ahead on the job. The truth is that these people may never make enough money or be satisfied with their status. They will always want something more. They may be restless and not know why. The locus of control for meaning and significance is internally located. Establish your core values and find your purpose to calm that savage beast that is constantly seeking more. ***Knowing who you are and what you are meant to do is what gives meaning and significance to your life.***

Recognise that humility is faith in action. Knowing that you are here to serve God and others puts perspective in your actions. Avoid acting on selfish impulses. Do not seek to thrive by using others or believing that you are better than they are. Examine your actions and try to understand the motive for doing whatever you are doing. Act from a position of love for humanity not out of wanting fame or fortune.

Be cognizant of your worth and value. You are blessed with certain skills, knowledge and talent. Use them but do not laud it over others for where you may be strong and they may be weak, you may be weak where they are strong. Recognise the strengths and accomplishments of others.

Even in the throes of a crisis situation, when it seems that your life may never be 'normal' again, it is possible to practice humility in some simple ways. In our society we like to do what is called "bad talking others". This refers to the practice of criticizing others. None of us are perfect. Simply eliminating this practice and starting a new practice of saying good things about others puts you one step closer to thriving forward. Another simple technique would be to accept criticism, take away what is instructive from such criticism and be grateful for the words of advice.

There are many simple ways of building humility into your daily life, even in difficult times. It takes some time and effort to keep from slipping into the old ways of acting and reacting. However with continuous striving for humility, keeping focus on others and not self, it gets easier to find ways to be humble.

Be Humble exercises

1. Submit all fears, concerns and sense of self-importance to God.
2. Be more compassionate and empathetic to others. Recognize the needs of others.
3. Graciously accept help, whether physical or emotional.
4. If you are faced with a job loss, put pride aside and do what is necessary, within moral and legal limits, to survive.
5. List your core values so that what you do is in alignment with your purpose.
6. Use your resources, limited or abundant, to serve others.

7. Put aside any perceived importance of your status and do for others. Start with simple things such as holding a door for someone or listening with full attention.

8. Look for the good in others so that your actions may bring out the best in them.

9. Refrain from undue criticism and learn to accept criticism graciously.

Key Learning Points

1. Humility involves serving God by serving others.
2. Humility removes the focus from self.
3. Humility is internally controlled: define your personal values and standards and know your purpose.
4. Make simple changes in your dealings with others to enhance humility and to forget self.

Step 8

BE FORGIVING

*"Enable resilience;
remove the shackles of
a lack of forgiveness."*

N OT BEING ABLE to forgive someone for some real or perceived ill that they may have done implies among other things, that you are infallible. It suggests that you believe that everything you do is right and that you can and have never done wrong. It reeks of a lack of humility. Human nature is imperfect. We are all capable of doing wrong at some point in time just as we are capable of being judgmental. However the injustice done in not forgiving yourself or others is just as or perhaps even worse than the precipitating act.

A lack of forgiveness triggers off a series of events. It leads to the accumulation of negative emotions on the part of the one harbouring resentment. This entrapment of anger and hurt has a two pronged danger. It cocoons negativity, causing it to be nurtured first by rehashing the act and then by rehearsing future possible actions.

Rehashing leads to your brain's video player rewinding and replaying the scene or event repeatedly. With each repetition, you become more incensed. The importance of the event grows. This leads to the intensity of your emotions becoming magnified. If left unchecked it begins to take control of you. This uncontrolled blossoming of anger, hurt and pain leads to thoughts of revenge, hatred and ultimately a complete breakdown of the relationship.

After my dad got ill late in November 2008 my mother and brothers adopted a pragmatic approach to his care. They selected palliative care. On the other hand, I felt we had to keep trying all that we could to treat him. Our polar approaches led to the development of a division between us that grew progressively worse until and even after his death.

For his funeral in 2009, one of my friends prepared a video with clips of pictures from different times of his life. The music accompanying the video was "The Last Farewell" by Roger Whittaker. I played that video over so many times that it got to the point where I would cry uncontrollably from the very first notes of the song, whether it was from my father's video or the radio. Of greater significance in hindsight, is that looking at that video compounded the anger I harboured against my mother and brothers. It got to the point where I had nothing to do with them until three years after his death.

Rehearsing on the other hand, involves carefully planning a series of alternative steps which may be taken in any future encounters with one who had done you wrong. Like rehashing, it too magnifies the importance of that situation of hurt. If the cycle of laying out alternative scenarios is not broken it may lead to corrosion of your soul, placing a limit on your happiness and ability to enjoy life. It may have even more dire consequences depending on factors such as your intellectual, moral, emotional and mental capacity.

Late in 2013 after the shooting incident, I was called for an interview with a representative from the Criminal Injuries Compensation Board. The interview was detail oriented. Documents such as the police report, the hospital report and all associated medical bills were presented. My physical injuries from the incident were obvious. Every detail about that egregious incident was reviewed. At the end of the interview I was informed of the process for the eventual granting of compensation which would involve a series of interviews before going before the Board members.

When I finally received a call to go up to the main office in Port of Spain, I was nervous and anxious. I cold sweated the night before, had nightmares and flashbacks and concocted a variety of scenarios each with its unique outcome. In some of the "rehearsals" I calmly stated my case; in other scenes I became emotional either crying or becoming angry. In none of the cases did I predict the final outcome.

On the following morning, I set out to our capital city, using the water taxi from San Fernando in South Trinidad. I arrived early and set out to locate the office. When I arrived at the office, I waited briefly before being escorted by a clerk to another office. As the morning unfolded none of the previously rehearsed enactments came through except the part where I broke down and started to cry. I cried with tears overflowing from brimming eyes at first but soon my entire body began to shake with emotion. I tried to calm myself before leaving but even as I descended in the elevator my face was washed with tears.

The crying did not stop until about half an hour later. It may have been a combination of factors including pent up emotion from the trauma of the past year. It may have been relief that at least one chapter in that turbulent period of my life was closed. It was over. C'est fini! Or maybe it could have been in part due to the rehearsing from the previous night. I had worked myself to a highly charged state which resulted in an avalanche of tears when the stress had been removed. Thus not being forgiving may lead to rehashing or rehearsing or both. These actions inevitably introduce an unprecedented and undesirable level of stress into your life.

On the other hand, adopting a forgiving posture is not an easy task. It requires a level of detachment and a large dose of humility. The ego must be able to let go of the weight of hurt, brought about by an injustice, otherwise that weight could begin to drag you down. The mighty things of this world: pride, status, wealth, need to be put into perspective in order for forgiveness to come more readily. Knowing that God is on your side; knowing that we all make mistakes; knowing that a lack of forgiveness, if left unchecked, is like a cancer that spreads rapidly consuming your entire being; knowing that forgiveness releases stress, frees you from being trapped by the past and gives you the impetus to move forward. Knowing all these things should reduce the emphasis placed on holding onto a grudge or a hurt.

I remember clearly the burning questions when I was interviewed at a breakfast meeting held by the Christian Chamber of Commerce in Oveido, Florida. The questions were "Have you forgiven the persons who did this to you? What would you say to them if you were to meet them face to face today?" I have to admit I surprised a few persons by my answer. It was a truthful answer yet unexpected.

My answer to that question then, and now, is that in as much as forgiveness is not really mine to give, I have forgiven the persons who committed this crime against me. I would like to let them know that there is a God and that God loves them as much as He loves everyone else. I had thought about that question many times before so the answer came easily for me that morning. I have forgiven. I harbour no thoughts of revenge. My only wish is that no one else is hurt by these perpetrators and that they may one day be reformed.

That said it does not mean that I have completely forgotten what happened or that I have minimized what happened. The enormity of that incident hits me every time I see my face, every time I touch my chin and I feel strange sensations. When I awake with a heaviness on my chin or feel like someone has slapped me on my face or when I am unable to properly chew foods or bite into a sandwich, when I have to repeat what I am trying to say because it comes out sounding garbled, I remember exactly what happened.

Working at this book, giving lessons, occasionally working part time and doing marketing for my first book all remind me of what took place that night. The ripple effect from that one incident is not lost on me. When my son is concerned about my leaving home ever again and is still battling with the trauma from that night, how can I forget or downplay the impact of that incident?

I may have forgiven by not wanting to hold on to thoughts of retribution or revenge but I have not forgotten. I do not know who did this to me. I have no idea what they look like. Yet when I am amongst a crowd I look around me suspiciously. It could have been anyone. As time goes by the paranoia grows less. As faith and forgiveness are allowed to do their work, I am able to move forward as it should be.

Be Forgiving Exercises

1. List at least one time you were hurt by the actions of someone and you did not forgive them. Recall how you felt immediately after the action and how you felt and reacted sometime after the incident.
2. List at least one time you were hurt and you did forgive. Recall how you felt immediately and sometime after the incident. Notice if you felt better after forgiving.
3. Recall at least one time you were the cause of hurt and pain to someone else. Did you feel sorry? Did you want forgiveness?
4. Be kind to yourself. Recall one incident for which you brought hurt and pain upon yourself. Consciously remind yourself that we are all imperfect and practice self-forgiveness.
5. When you get angry practice breathing deeply, go for a walk or run, spend time with a pet, listen to music, write in a journal or do something you like to release the negative energy.
6. List possible reasons why you or someone else may have done an injustice to try to understand the action.
7. Daily and deliberately forgive at least one person for even a minor wrong to help develop the habit of forgiveness.

Key Learning Points

1. A forgiving attitude acknowledges your humanity, your imperfections.
2. To be able to forgive requires humility.
3. A lack of forgiveness is compounded by two actions: rehearsing and rehashing.
4. Forgiveness brings you one step closer to releasing the past and moving forward.

Step 9

CONTINUOUSLY STRIVE
TO IMPROVE

*"Poise for higher rebounding
by a commitment to life-long learning."*

SOMETIME IN 2016, I attended a career guidance workshop as a chaperone to some students. At the workshop, the feature speaker shared his story with the students. His story was simple but quite inspirational. He told them his story of having the basic subjects upon leaving school. He explained that even though he was not initially qualified, he knew with which company he wanted to work. This conclusion he had arrived at because he knew that working there would earn him the amount of money he needed to support his dream lifestyle.

He set about getting a job at the company by systematically improving his knowledge and skills base and acquiring the certification to prove it. He did many short courses and when he finally got an interview his drive, ambition and urgent desire to get the job all worked in his favour to win him that coveted position. According to him, the interviewer saw the "hunger in his eyes" for the job and knew that he would be the perfect fit when that passion was combined with his qualifications.

In addition to setting goals, as was outlined in Step One, the gentleman had the passion, the determination and the drive to do what it took to achieve what he envisioned. He was willing to spend the time, money and effort needed to invest in his education for self-improvement.

Let me share my own story. During my younger years I obtained full ordinary and advanced level certificates at the secondary school level. I went on to obtain a Bachelor and Master of Science Degree. But that was not all I did. I did a short counselling course with a religious group. I volunteered at ALTA(Adult Literacy Training Association) in Trinidad. I completed a computer course on basic programming (a very long time ago). Later on I continued to do many short courses related to teaching and chemistry before completing the Diploma in Education.

After the incident it would have been so easy to stop doing anything but I was "hungry", just like the young speaker was. So when my recuperation was well on the way, I did many different things to acquire new knowledge and skills. The technology now, compared to when I was younger, makes it easy to improve, if you choose so to do.

I started with a free online mediation course because I had become passionate about restorative justice. Restorative justice has many merits but that is for another forum. I read about and began practicing mindfulness meditation. I read many motivational and inspirational books. I even read books on sales and marketing. I began to keep a journal and eventually wrote and published my own book. I attended two preaching seminars and had several speaking engagements. I share this with you for the sole purpose of highlighting the need to constantly improve. I am emulating this trait because it is one that many successful persons have in common. They strive continuously to be better.

Another aspect of improving yourself is being able to listen to and implement changes as a result of **constructive** criticism (take note of the word in bold letters). One of the most difficult things to do, at least for me, is to listen to criticism. Particularly when I was younger, I was thin-skinned. Criticism hurt and I reacted angrily toward the deliverer of the message on many occasions. Through the vicissitudes of time, I have learnt to be more appreciative of negative comments.

I have learnt to listen without interruption or bias. I have learnt to accept that not everyone will like or understand what I am doing or how I choose to do it. I have learnt that someone's opinion is just that – their opinion. It does not mean that I am wrong or that what I have done is bad but that it is different to what someone else may do or expect. Most importantly I have learnt that, upon reflection, what at first may seem to be harsh and without merit, may prove to have wisdom and I have learnt to act on that wisdom.

If you want to be able to bounce back successfully from an upheaval, minor or major, or if you just want to accomplish a particular goal, then I highly recommend that you challenge yourself to embark on a journey of lifelong learning. Become certified in areas that will supplement your goals. Keep reading widely. Listen to others to help guide your improvement but not at the expense of your individuality.

Intellectual improvement ought not to be an excuse for abandonment of values, compassion, gentleness and love. Too many times I have seen self-professed intellectuals with inflated egos, acting harshly towards others. The sad part is that many so-called educators fall into that trap of a magnified sense of self. There have always been and continue to be persons in positions of authority who abuse those who fall under their jurisdiction. They berate others, diminishing their self-esteem.

By improving yourself through continuous learning, you are being proactive about resilience building. What you do, apart from acquiring new knowledge and skills, is that you provide for yourself release valves. The release valves are mechanisms you put in place to help in coping with difficulties. By indulging in learning, the burden of a trial is, at least temporarily, pushed out of focus. When this is done for a period of time, the perceived enormity of the burden evolves into something more manageable.

An approach to lifelong learning puts things into perspective. It allows you to see the bigger picture, recognizing that your trial is transient. It allows you to adopt a long term approach to life, accepting any challenge as a chance for change, seeing it for what it is: an unanticipated opportunity.

Had I not been continuously reading about health issues, nutrition and supplementation throughout most of my adult life, I may have depended entirely on doctors and nurses for my recovery. The knowledge I had gleaned over the years and put into active practice paid off for me at that critical time in my life, my defining moment. Once I was past the critical stage, I was able to take responsibility for my recovery, without being totally dependent on the medical staff. To be clear, their contribution was invaluable. I could not have pulled through without their professional expertise. However, with the doctors having paved the road to recovery, the onus was on me to commit to practices that would enhance their efforts. These practices would result from a blending of general knowledge of health and intimate knowledge of my body and its peculiar biochemistry.

Find something you like to do or something that you are good at or something you always wanted to do and get started with it. Give your recreational pursuit full attention and commitment. For me, jogging or walking is stress relieving, leaves me physically tired yet rejuvenated and helps me sweat out toxins. It also produces endorphins and alleviates the dark clouds of depression.

You may prefer a less energetic pursuit such as reading or playing a musical instrument. Another person may enjoy dancing or Zumba! Whatever works for you, whatever activity you are able to sustain diligently, that is the pastime for you. Be more adventurous; try hiking, zip-lining or scuba-diving. Join a debating club or do karaoke.

In Step 3 I mentioned about the formation of new neural pathways. Indulging in learning and doing new activities, creates networks which in turn engage areas of the brain that tend to become less functional as we age. These new connections help combat memory loss, slowed reactions and other cognitive losses associated with aging. In addition, doing and learning create mental check valves to release excessive stress leaving you empowered for faster, better recovery. Wouldn't you want to be able to bounce back better after a difficulty or to adjust more quickly to a new normal?

Continuously Strive to Improve Exercises

1. Consider if your qualifications match your purpose or mission. If they do not, or if they do but can be enhanced, then list all the steps you can take to more effectively position yourself to accomplish your purpose.
2. Select one item in your list from (1) with which to get started.
3. Apart from those in (1), list at least 5 other courses, certificates, degrees or topics that you always thought about doing or caught your interest at some time. Select one and enroll as soon as possible.
4. Keep working on the two lists: cross off items and add more items.
5. Heed criticism and do self-analysis and research to determine its relevance before making adjustments.
6. Begin reading a new book.
7. Try a new fun activity.

Key Learning Outcomes

1. Spend time, money and effort for self-improvement.
2. Listen to others and implement constructive criticism.
3. Adopt a coach or mentor.
4. Marry intellectual improvement with sound morals and values.

Step 10

PRACTICE PHILANTHROPY

"No matter how little you have,
you have more than someone else.
Give as you strive forward."

ANY HIGHLY REGARDED persons have espoused the virtues
of doing for others. Rotarians internationally promote the
act of service to others. Albert Einstein identified the act
of service as the greatest act one could perform. Jesus Christ gave His
life for all of us- the ultimate act of service. Giving of self to others is
a virtue to be emanated, a chance to show love for humanity and an
opportunity for growth and happiness.

I remember one day being despondent about my financial and social
situation. I had recently bought a new car and acquired an old house.
My loan payments per month were staggering on a single income. I had
very few friends and the one person who I considered more than a friend
appeared not to have the capacity to empathize or perhaps did not care
enough to do so. It was one of the times that I felt lonely.

That day I set out to immerse myself in doing household chores
starting with painting the gate at the front of my yard. I love painting
because I can indulge in a lot of thought as I paint. I became self-
absorbed as I painted the gate. I slipped into deeper thoughts with
every stroke of the brush and as the sun beamed down relentlessly with
increasing intensity, I had one more reason to feel sorry for myself. Alone
with perspiration dripping as I labored in the mid-morning sun, I forgot

about gratitude and appreciation; I forgot about responsibility and the benefits of physical activity. In fact my attitude was so negative, that I became myopic to the many good things in my life; things that I took for granted that others may not have had.

Steeped in self-pity, I was startled when an elderly man who occupied an abandoned house in the neighbourhood stopped to say good morning. He was out on his daily routine of looking for odd jobs and collecting discarded items to re-sell. I responded to his greeting in a dejected voice, still wallowing in self-pity. Detecting my mood, he sought to lift my spirits by speaking words of encouragement and spiritual advice.

Even in my self-absorbed state I was able to appreciate what he was trying to do. Here was a man, himself in a destitute situation, rising to the challenge of imbuing hope to one whom he perceived as being in greater need than he was. He walked away, in the blistering, almost mid-day sunlight, with a cheerful demeanor and a hearty, "alright, you have a good day eh." My mood lightened although I felt a twinge of guilt for having been so inwardly focused.

The takeaway here is that, even if the world may see you as having nothing to give, you do have something more than at least one other person at any given time. Holding on to what you have serves no purpose. It does not grow in value. It does not bring hope, or peace or happiness. In fact it just sits with you and soon could become forgotten. Putting what you have to use, especially to help someone else, increases its value; it may bring hope to someone else and bring you peace and happiness.

When you are faced with adversity, it is easy to focus only on what you do not have and how bad your situation appears to be. The truly resilient people are those who are able to *know* what their situation is but to lay it aside for a while and place emphasis on others. They spend time with others, they do things for others, they give of their material things to others and they do it with no expectations.

Many companies now give back. They do it out of a sense of

corporate social responsibility. The rewards to them are both tangible and immeasurable. There are monetary gains, popularity and free advertisements for example. But there is also the joy and camaraderie achieved upon giving and doing for others. The hard work involved in planning and execution is all worth the while upon seeing the positive effect on the lives of those who needed the assistance.

In my own case, when I was cash strapped, looking for assistance for reconstructive surgery, many individuals and some institutions came forward to help. One company, which had made a substantial contribution in my estimation, was Methanex Trinidad Limited.

The greatness of this gesture lay in several facts:

1. I was not associated with the company.
2. No conditions were applied to the donation.
3. No fanfare or publicity was made about the grant.
4. At my lowest time financially, I received assistance.

With the cash received from Methanex as well as other sources, I was able to comfortably meet my medical expenses. The seed for a new relationship was planted. When I launched my first book, Methanex Trinidad Limited was among the first to receive a copy, as an act of my gratitude. Their generosity in part helped to bring me back to a semblance of my former self.

One of the best stories on giving is one I read about the veterinarian, Dr. Kryiann Singh, who was mentioned in Step 2, Feel, Grieve, Accept. It was the first of many stories on his acts of service that I had heard. That story began several years ago; he had responded to a house call at night to help in the delivery of a calf. The cow was having some difficulty and because of where the cow was located and the time of night, no other vet was willing to go. Dr. Singh agreed to go but on the condition that he would be lifted up and taken to the cow. Remember he could not go on his own as he was a paraplegic owing to an accident some years prior to that night.

That night he did his best. As he worked with the cow, the owner's daughter got ill. He urged the owner to leave him and take the daughter to seek medical assistance. Further when he had completed the job he told the man's wife that no payment was necessary; instead he told her to use the money to pay for the child's medical treatment. He left that night satisfied with having done a good job and not expecting anything in return.

Fast forward years later, the vet was tired after a difficult day. On his way home he saw a vegetable stall. He stopped to purchase one item asking for assistance as it would be cumbersome for him to come out on the side of the road, given his disability. The vendor agreed to help him, offering other vegetables. The vet, upon seeing how fresh the veggies looked, happily agreed to take whatever was offered. Soon his car was filled with much produce, good wholesome food.

When he had as much as he could possibly need, he asked for the bill. The vendor, a young lady, told him there would be no charge. As he argued, the girl's father suddenly appeared. The father reminded the vet of his kindness to them many years ago when he had attended to their birthing cow. His act of kindness and generosity many years ago had come full circle back to him. Although we ought not to give to get, the story is heartwarming.

Giving removes the focus from your own problems or adversity. It gives new meaning and purpose to a less than fulfilling life. Giving stimulates the production of "feel good" hormones such as dopamine; it makes the giver feel better and of course the recipient has a need fulfilled. Dopamine stimulation results in the giver wanting to give more as they begin to feel more.

In the midst of experiencing a meltdown in December 2013 having been diagnosed with Post Traumatic Stress Disorder, I did something that I am convinced helped speed up recovery. I was having flashbacks, nightmares, crying episodes, oversleeping and avoiding company. I had to deal with the after effects of all the surgery. There were the numerous stares whenever I did go out. To top it all off, I now had no income; my salary had been stopped after continuous leave in excess of six months according to the policy of the Ministry of Education of Trinidad and Tobago.

In keeping with a practice I, along with a co-worker, had cultivated with our students in years past, I donated grocery items to two families. The acts of going to purchase the items, of thinking about what the families would most need and of trying to guess what would be unexpected and bring an extra burst of happiness to them was the most amazing therapy for me. I was able to shift the burden of my own pain and sadness to joy and fulfillment by doing for and giving to others.

I have never met those who were the recipients of my gifts. The donations were done through the San Fernando General Hospital Psychiatric Clinic, the clinic where I had been receiving treatment and counselling for the PTSD. I can only imagine the temporary relief they would have felt. But that act brought me one step closer to healing. It reinforced my efforts to regain control of my life. *I was finding myself by losing myself in service to others.* By consciously acting with love and in faith against the tidal wave of depression, I was building resilience. I was positioning myself to bounce back better.

We are all capable of doing this.

Practice Philanthropy Exercises

1. Practice one selfless act today.
2. Spend time with an elderly or lonely person.
3. Offer transport to someone who does not have easy access to transport.
4. Help a friend or neighbor with a chore.
5. Pay the grocery or pharmacy bill for someone who cannot afford it.
6. Prepare a meal for a sick or grieving person or family.
7. Join a charitable organization and be an active member.
8. Form a charitable organization and be active.

Key Learning Points

1. Knowing that adversity and pain are inevitable, prepare for such times by making service and generosity a part of your daily life.
2. Be more compassionate at all times, to all persons.
3. In difficult times reduce the burden of your challenge by taking your attention away from it and placing that attention on doing for others.
4. Bounce back better by striving to be altruistic – lose yourself in service to others.

Step 11

BE REFLECTIVE

*"Reflecting sheds light on dark corners of your mind,
bringing release, appreciation and growth
to help you thrive against all odds."*

LOVE RUNNING. WHEN I run, I think, I reflect on my day, on my week, on my run and on my life. If something disturbed me during the day, reflecting on it while I run is a surefire way to ease the burden of that disturbance. I love writing, maybe not as much as running but I love writing. When I write, I have to think. I reflect on my day, on my week, on what I am writing and on my life. I remove the clutter from my mind and put it onto the paper. The paper does not judge me. It does not run to tell its nearest listening ear my thoughts.

When I was unable to speak after being shot, I wrote a lot. I wrote to communicate with family, friends, nurses and doctors when they came to see me or if I needed something. I also wrote to get rid of thoughts that were beginning to crowd my little mind. Removing those thoughts from the abstract and transforming them into something tangible worked like waving a magic wand. I gained insight that was not always easily detectable. I was able to discern what was really important and discard what could have hampered my progress.

After being discharged from hospital, I had to face reality. I was unable to move back to my own home as I would need someone to assist me until I had regained some strength. All parties who had shown solidarity by visiting with me at the hospital now had to settle back into their normal routines which did not include a daily visit to see me. I had to deal with being at home when everyone else was going back to work. I had to be around my family, seeing them eating food, food which I was unable to eat. Everything that was once familiar now seemed so different, daunting and difficult.

There were nights of restlessness and sleeplessness. Dark memories shot into my mind at odd times. I grew weaker as the days went by – I could not eat and drinking food was not my idea of a meal. There were so many heavy thoughts to deal with; thoughts that could not be shared with anyone else; thoughts that could threaten my sanity if they were not released. One evening, in a desperate attempt to clear those all-consuming mental images, I began to write. At first the words were jumbled. Thoughts were written as they entered my mind…chaotic writings from a confused mind.

As the weeks passed by the writing moved from stumbling and ranting to greater clarity and certainty. Thoughts began to flow in some semblance of order. The ritual of sitting down to write became a vital part of the entire writing process. The place I chose to sit and write assumed profound importance. I had to locate myself to secure minimum disturbance, where I could rise into a cloud of thought and float away into the deepest parts of my psyche. One evening as I was exploring the internet, I re-discovered an old blog in which I had written either one or two posts some years earlier. Filled with excitement, I wrote my first blog post after the incident.

This accomplishment, minor as it may seem to the average person, was a major breakthrough for me. I could assume anonymity and communicate with the world! That produced a sense of euphoria and exhilaration. I now had at least one task to look forward to daily. This gave me a sense of purpose and it helped to relieve the burden of those heavily weighted thoughts that had begun to accumulate. I wrote about things in my past. I wrote about what had happened to me. I shared my feelings of despair, depression and desperation.

An amazing transformation began to envelope me. As I wrote, I gained more clarity both in my thoughts and in the direction in which my life was heading. As a result, the vision for a book, based on the incident was born and I started to write furiously…until I hit that proverbial wall with which marathoners are familiar. To my mind, the story was not making sense. There seemed to be no substance to it. The format did not cater to teach anything of value. I realized I was just sharing a story and I felt I needed to do something more than that. No matter how hard I tried at that time I could not get past the story. The harder I tried to incorporate lessons the more elusive those lessons became. I eventually put aside thoughts of writing a book for what would be the next seven months and instead, focused on blogging about feelings, fears and the future.

The benefit gained from writing and running was that these activities encouraged me to spend many hours reflecting. Reflecting on life in general and on your life in particular brings enlightenment. It illuminates those corners in the mind that were either forgotten or never used. It reveals choices that could be made when in other difficult situations yet to be faced. It forces you to come to terms with and appreciate what has been, to learn from the past and to apply principles from the past to enhance the present and future.

One day, I reflected on the time I had spent on Ward Eight at San Fernando General Hospital. I remembered looking at the news on the television that was directly facing my bed. Sometimes I could not hear what was being said but that night I was hearing quite well. An interview was in progress with a young girl diagnosed with Cerebral Palsy. Her appearance and condition could easily create the judgment that she was not intelligent, that nothing was going on mentally for her but she spoke about how much she had to offer intellectually and her speech, though not perfectly coherent, was brilliant.

Her words resonated within me because I too had become a victim of judgment owing to my appearance. Because I could not speak and because of the large bandages on my face, many persons visiting felt the need to speak to me as if I were intellectually challenged. Internally, I cringed every time someone felt they had to reassure me that all would be well and that God was trying to teach me a lesson. It grated against my senses when, with eyes filled with pity, someone would speak to me slowly, loudly and in a manner which suggested that they thought I was a simpleton (perhaps they were being truthful for the first time). I wanted to shout out that my brain was not damaged; I could not speak but that did not mean I could not hear and understand.

Upon reflection I realized that I too was being judgmental. These persons themselves did not know how to cope with what was happening and perhaps could not cope if they had been in my situation. They were offering all that they could have offered to me at the time. Empathy was, and still is, in short supply. It is something we need to consciously cultivate, for without empathy how can we genuinely feel for others and with others?

Reflecting shines light equally on the positive and negative aspects of the past placing emphasis on what is truly important. Sometimes we all want to forget the bad things that happen to us. We are told to focus on the positive but the truth is that, "we are the sum total of our experiences" as my mentor and friend, Mr. Raymond Hackett, has reiterated on many occasions. Who we are today is a result of all that has happened to us in the past. We learn from the good and the bad. However, we seem to learn more from the bad.

Resilience requires that we embrace the bad along with the good times and use all our experiences in striving toward a life of meaning and purpose. Resilient people recognize that there are lessons to be learnt from their experiences, all of their experiences, and even the experiences of those around them. They are willing to indulge in profound analysis of past events. However hurtful the process, they usually emerge with a wealth of tools, lessons and stories which will support them as they bounce back into their new reality.

Sometimes we develop latent skills or acquire new skills when we have no choice but to be creative in dealing with a difficult situation. When the crisis is over, the skill may not be needed again...until the next time adversity strikes. Reflection is a form of revision. It helps to transfer learnt skills or knowledge from short term memory to long term memory. The next time there is a need for action when under pressure or stress, the practice of reflection will make it easier for you to recall the previously learnt and adequately stored information and to transfer the principles learnt to a different situation.

In the heat of the moment, things are said and done which may have a resoundingly good effect or which may have a bitter after-effect. It is only when reflection has taken place that we are able to determine how the situation made us feel, how any other parties involved may have felt, what could have been done differently and what we can learn from the situation. This in-depth thinking provides the advantage of insight to one who engages in reflection. Indeed, reflection reveals where emotion may have been allowed to take control and where reason and compassion ought to have been applied.

Reflection as a practice helps in increasing self-awareness. Self-awareness in turn is a trait of resilient persons; it is vital for functioning from a healthy psychological platform. To come to the point of accepting external events in our life that impact upon the internal self, it is essential to allow thoughts about the situation to trickle through the various filters in the mind to separate emotions from facts thereby creating useful nuggets to promote recovery or re-establish a form of normalcy.

Be Reflective Exercises

1. Find a quiet place to mull over your thoughts, feelings and actions.
2. Go to the beach, take a walk or run or do whatever activity makes you relax. Relaxation promotes the right conditions for reflection.
3. Exercise regularly for stimulation and preparation for reflection.

4. Start a journal, even with one sentence daily, as you become relaxed.

5. Become more aware of your surroundings, your feelings and the feelings of others and the actions of others and yourself – practice mindfulness.

6. When next you are feeling angry or are in a negative situation: stop, stand back and observe yourself. Why do you feel angry? Have you ever felt like this before? What did you do the last time you felt angry like this? Did your reaction then help you to feel better or to resolve the problem?

7. Use the questioning technique as in the exercise above to analyse any type of situation.

Key Learning Points

1. Ease the burden of difficulties by reflecting.
2. Reflection involves analysis of our feelings and actions – as well as feelings and actions of others.
3. Being able to genuinely let go of the past so as to thrive requires growth that comes through reflection.
4. Insight to self and others is gained through reflection.

CONCLUSION

"We are troubled on every side, yet not distressed;
we are perplexed, but not in despair;
Persecuted, but not forsaken; cast down, but not destroyed;"
2 Corinthians 4: 8 – 9 KJV

W E ALL FACE challenges, custom made for each of us; designed to fit our personalities, our circumstances, and our levels of resilience. With reference to the scripture above, though the troubles faced in those times were different from ours, the gist of the message is the same. There is always trouble, in different forms and intensities and likewise, there is always hope. The challenge one person faces may seem larger than that faced by someone else but nobody's hurt and pain should be minimized by another. What seems easy for you in your particular circumstance may be traumatizing for someone else under their peculiar circumstances.

In times of tribulation, we are left with two choices: adopt a negative attitude or develop a positive approach. A negative attitude characteristically leaves us paralysed with hurt, bitterness and anger. Moving on with life would be like trying to lift a truck – a task of daunting proportions. On the other hand, choosing a positive approach cultivates acceptance, well-being, faith, humility, self- improvement and philanthropy and removes obstacles like revenge, lack of forgiveness and ingratitude- all of which can hamper growth and the ability to push off past afflictions.

Let us compare life to a marathon. We start off life full of energy, ready and rearing to go. Similarly, the runner has trained for the marathon and is confident of being able to finish the race regardless of the conditions he has yet to face. As the horn is sounded at the start of the race, he sets out at a reasonable pace, already calculated, after all he is approaching this race scientifically. Suddenly a few kilometres into the race, he feels an unfamiliar twitching in his lower leg muscles. It persists and is uncomfortable. He has to slow down his pre-calculated pace, knowing that he could incur injury if he does not and, at the same time, fully aware that if he does, his race time may suffer severely. He does what he has to do to keep moving in a manner that will ensure he completes the race, all things taken into consideration.

After a while the discomfort either is forgotten or has gone away. Whatever is the reason, he is back on track. Step by step he pounds away on course, gradually picking up the pace having mentally re-calculated to try to stay close to his original plan. Over and over, before he crosses the finish line, he experiences setbacks and recovery periods; he re-calibrates, slowing down and speeding up repeatedly. He aches, he thirsts, he perspires, he thinks and he focusses.

To the onlooker he appears to be running, just running. Tired, running, sweaty; that is what the crowd sees: him, a runner, straining to meet the finish line, plodding along, one step at a time. When the line is crossed, the runner appears to be aloof and snobbish. He glances at the time, grimacing or smiling as he pushes everyone out of his way, heading for water, rest and food.

His exhilaration begins to set in. He has done it! He has fought against the wind, the pains, the challenges and he has emerged victorious. He did not place first or second or even third, but he has finished. He has finished and has achieved! Perhaps he got a finisher's medal or perhaps he did not, but he persevered and he completed the race that was set before him, despite the obstacles along the way.

Life is like a marathon. We start off in innocence, with energy and excitement about everything. We have dreams and visions and set out to accomplish these. Along the way we battle against the winds of challenges, sometimes having to slow down or divert from our goals as we take up arms against these winds. The great thing is that if we do not lose heart, if we persist and plod along step by step, keeping our focus on positive goals, then one day we cross our finish line emerging polished to a glistening sheen by the frictional forces of adversity.

The marathoner of today approaches his training and race with scientific precision and bamboo-like flexibility. The journey of life ought to be traversed in a similar manner. I have shared my stories of recovery from a dramatic, traumatic experience in my life with you. I have described how I was able to:

1. Plan for the long term but...
2. Grieve and accept the situation
3. Embrace it by living in the moment
4. Be prepared to move on by developing physically
5. Lean on strong support systems
6. Submit to a higher order and develop faith
7. Be humble, recognizing my place in this life
8. Practice forgiveness to free myself from a self-imposed prison
9. Use continuous learning to propel me forward
10. Deflect the negative effect of my situation by giving to others
11. Internalize, analyze and thrive by reflection.

By utilizing one of the key learning points, reflection, I was able to document for you the systematic method which I followed in order to detour from one path along my life's journey to another. That diversion allowed me to push past the hurt and the pain of an unforeseen obstacle, into unexplored territory. It was a process through which humility, courage, perseverance and faith helped me to circumvent the destined adversity, strategically placed into the drama that is life.

The step by step method I have shared with you worked and is still working for me. It may work for you too, if you take the time to follow the steps as I have laid them out. Pain and hurt may be unavoidable but our resilience levels are much greater than we are sometimes aware. Of greater significance is the capacity to build resilience: a capacity that we all have and can bring into play by implementing the steps I have shared.

Many of the steps are proactive as well as reactive. None of us should expect to traverse this journey of life without encountering some degree of difficulty. Difficult times are to be expected but we can never know exactly when nor can we always predict what the nature of it may be. The one thing we are sure of is that it will happen. Armed with that knowledge, it is our responsibility to prepare ourselves for the inevitable negative twist in our fate. We ought to be able to transfer the practices which worked in good times to get them working again in bad times. But even if we sailed through life with so few storms that we took for granted the spontaneity of adversity, these steps may still be applied to bring us out of the darkness of despair.

Preparation for any future change, negative or positive, requires having a vision and a mission. It entails knowing your purpose or at least seeking it out. Goals, long term and short term, need to be set. Setting these goals requires being realistic and time oriented but it also requires bamboo-like flexibility; it means knowing that anything can happen at any time requiring a change in your plan of action. The bamboo plant is known to be so flexible that it may bend to great angles without breaking in the wind, bouncing back to an upright position when the wind dies down.

So too we need to be able to adjust when the winds of change blow, laying low until the wind has passed; we need to accept what has happened. Coming to acceptance means allowing both negative and positive feelings to be experienced. It does not mean adopting a defeatist attitude. Instead we feel and process our feelings so that we are able to come to terms with our situation.

In difficult times, we have examined the benefits of living in the moment. This simply means we appreciate every second of the day, living in a slowed down version of reality until we have the capacity to emerge stronger and better.

Although we cannot fully prepare for that of which we do not know, we can take control of that which we know and which belongs to us. This means we can take steps to strengthen our bodies and minds in good times so that should a spontaneous negative event occur, we will have the physical, mental and emotional stamina and resilience from which to draw. This calls for good nutrition practices and commitment to an exercise programme.

The value we place on relationships is vital in any recovery process. It is important for every one of us to be taught or to learn for ourselves the importance of familial and social relationships. Human nature is such that people are always around and supportive in good times. It is only those priceless, nurtured relationships that make it through the foggy struggles of difficult times. Without support that is genuine and constructive, the recovery period from any type of challenge tends to be longer. I have come to appreciate the strength of a good support network and am still in the process of learning to develop and use support systems. Many people already have cultivated nurturing relationships upon which they can depend in times of difficulty. If you do not, there is hope. It is not too late to start reaching out to others and lending support to others.

Likewise faith is a vital cog in the machinery of resilience. We can never reach saturation point in terms of faith. Neither can you declare another's faith to be less than yours nor can you say that yours is greater than another's. Faith is by nature extremely personal. It is an intimate relationship between you and God. (Those who consider themselves more enlightened refer to this as a relationship between you and the Universe. The choice is yours. I choose to develop faith with God). Out of faith come human kindnesses which contribute to character and the ability to bounce back better.

Faith requires a loss of self-focus and a redirection to others. This in turn promotes the practices of humility, forgiveness and philanthropy; all of which are lubricants for the cog in the resilience machine. Further enhancement in resilience may be achieved by a lifelong commitment to self- improvement.

Combining all these factors with reflection yields an attitude of overcoming and appreciation which can buttress significantly the physical, emotional and mental framework of resilience.

We live in extremely stressful and difficult times. The challenges we face are of the same nature faced from time immemorial, but now they are fueled by technological advances. To survive in a world filled with all manners of turbulence and to be able to rise victoriously above the threatening whirlpools of adversity, one has to have a system. Just as a scientist systematically analyses an unknown to determine its identity, we have to systematically chip away at the layers of hurt, frustration and fear to determine our courage, strength and perseverance.

The nightmare of trauma is a demon to be conquered. No battle can be won without being prepared and properly armed. Armed with self-awareness, acceptance, a fixed routine, a hobby and the possibility of professional help, this psychological and somatic battle can be won.

The waves of negativity and its fallout can be switched off with some diligence. Its spontaneous destruction can be avoided with courage using a ruthless and relentless strategy consisting of all the steps outlined above.

"The imperfections created by my past experiences
may seem unsightly to others.
But… they are my trophies and my crowning glory,
Reminding me daily of the struggles I have
endured and have yet to face,
The tenacity I have developed through coping with my trials and
the strength and beauty of resilience."

BIBLIOGRAPHY

1. Preamble to the Constitution of the World Health Organization as adopted by the International Health Conference, New York, 19-22 June, 1946; signed on 22 July 1946 by the representatives of 61 States (Official Records of the World Health Organization, no. 2, p. 100) and entered into force on 7 April 1948.

2. The Science of Sleep. Accessed May 2016. http://healthysleep.med.harvard.edu/healthy/science

3. Hayes, Steven C., and Spencer Smith. Get Out of Your Mind & Into Your Life. The New Acceptance & Commitment Therapy. California: New Harbinger Publications, Inc., 2005.

ABOUT THE AUTHOR

CARON ASGARALI IS a survivor who has overcome tremendous adversity. She was the victim of a criminal act of violence in 2013 during an attempted robbery in the island of Trinidad.

She has since published her first book, From Lion to Lamb, A Spiritual Journey.

Caron was a Chemistry teacher before the incident, with a fiercely independent approach to life. She always believed in personal responsibility for physical, emotional, mental and spiritual health. She was able to use her commitment to health and education to shift from striving after the attack to thriving.

Her scientific background proved to be invaluable as she used a systematic approach to navigate her way through multiple setbacks encountered after being shot.

As an educator, Caron is committed to sharing the principles involved in building resilience that helped her along the way to bouncing back better.

More Books by Caron Asgarali

Do you want to embark on a journey,

guided by the hand of God, through the labyrinth of despair to the shore of hope?

Is it your desire to emerge victorious from the stranglehold of adversity? Then walk in the footsteps of a gunshot victim and experience the austerity of physical and spiritual recuperation!

In this book, *From Lion to Lamb: A Spiritual Journey*, you will learn lessons, influenced by the Sermon on the Mount, on

- Faith and submission
- Empathy and magnanimity
- Hope and courage
- The promise of greater glory

"Caron gives her message in simple and clear terms, promoting such Universal principles as love, peace, kindness..., *From Lion to Lamb* is well worth reading."

—Philip G. Rochford, Author and empowerment strategist

CARON R. ASGARALI is a Chemistry teacher in the Republic of Trinidad and Tobago. She was the victim of a violent crime (wounding with intent) in January, 2013. She shares her story as a means of imbuing hope to others.

RELIGION / Christian Life / Inspirational

V1.0

outskirts press

OutskirtsPress.com

U.S. $XX.XX

CARON ASGARALI

Foreword By Philip G. Rochford, HBM Author and Empowerment Strategist

From

LION
to
LAMB
A Spiritual Journey

FROM LION TO LAMB

CARON ASGARALI

Contact Caron Asgarali

If you have any questions, comments or would like to talk to Caron, you may contact her at:

caron_asgarali@yahoo.com
or call her at
1-868-370-4086.

Please visit
https://wwwamazon.com
to leave a review on this book, Bounce Back Better, or visit
https://www.amazon.com/
Lion-Lamb-Spiritual-Journey/dp/1478733616
to leave a review on her first book,
From Lion to Lamb, A Spiritual Journey.

Printed in the United States
By Bookmasters